This Book Belongs To:

The Sunshine Box

Written and Illustrated by
Millicent Moss

GOLD 'N' HONEY BOOKS   SISTERS, OREGON

THE SUNSHINE BOX
published by Gold 'n' Honey Books
a division of Multnomah Publishers, Inc.

© 1998 by Millicent Moss

Illustrations ©1998 by Millicent Moss

Design by Susan Luckey Higdon

International Standard Book Number: 1-57673-132-4

Printed in Hong Kong

To Ben, the best big brother
a sister could ever have…
and in memory of our dear parents,
who gave us such a treasured childhood

Table of Contents

Chapter 1

A DAY OF BIG EXPECTATIONS

*T*he early morning sun shone through Millie's open window and gently woke her from a pleasant sleep. She listened to the distant cock-a-doodle-doo of a rooster, followed by the songs of the sparrows in the nearby maple tree. Brushing tousled hair from her eyes, ten-year-old Millie yawned and stretched. For a moment she remained still, her head cushioned by her feather pillow. Then suddenly she remembered what day it was.

Millie hopped out of bed and ran to her older brother's bedroom.

"Benjamin, Benjamin!" she called. "Wake up! Only one more day until school starts!"

"Millie," grumbled Benjamin, "did you wake me up just to tell me that?" Groaning, he turned over and burrowed deeper into the rumpled covers.

"But, Benjamin," said Millie, nudging the pile of blankets, "we have so much to do today. We've got to get ready for tomorrow!"

"Maybe you have a lot to do, Millie, but this is the last day of summer vacation." Suddenly Benjamin's face brightened and he leaped out of bed. "The last day of vacation? I'm going fishing!"

Millie watched in wonder as he snatched up his clothes. Why, he wasn't even a bit excited about the first day of school!

For the past few weeks, Millie had been happily occupied getting ready for the first day of school. She and Mamma had already made several trips to town to buy what Millie and twelve-year-old Benjamin needed. Clothes had been Mamma's first concern. The long, hot days of summer would soon be gone, and with winter fast approaching, they would need heavy clothing to keep them warm.

About a month ago, Mamma had driven their shiny red Chevrolet sedan down the country road to town. Their first stop had been the fabric store. After looking carefully through the many bolts of fabric, Mamma said, "This blue wool would make a nice jumper for you, Millie." Mamma ran her hand across the thick piece of cloth.

"But Mamma, look!" Millie said as she pointed to some fabric behind the counter. Delicate blue and white flowers stood out against the bright red background. "Isn't that pretty?"

"That is pretty, Millie, but our weather will soon turn cold. That fabric wouldn't keep you very warm," explained Mamma. "Look over here at these nice soft plaids. They're colorful and would make a warm skirt. Why don't you choose one?"

Millie shrugged her shoulders and reluctantly turned from the lovely floral fabric to look at the plaids. She chose one in yellow and blue that was quite pretty, and decided plaid might not be so bad after all.

Millie enjoyed watching Mamma sew the fabric into clothes. One rainy afternoon as Mamma worked on the new plaid skirt she said, "Look at all these leftover scraps. Perhaps you could make a warm bedcover for your rag doll. Fabric scraps should never be wasted." Mamma always had such wonderful ideas! She helped Millie spread out the pieces on the kitchen table. Millie cut out small squares from the bits of cloth, and Mamma showed her how to stitch them together. As Millie worked, the squares slowly grew into a miniature quilt that just fit Millie's doll bed.

The following week, Mamma was very busy. Some vegetables from their garden still needed to be picked and canned. Because of the war President Roosevelt had urged people to grow "victory gardens." Papa plowed up a big plot in back, and Mamma and Benjamin planted the seeds. The rest of the summer, Mama, Benjamin, and Millie had faithfully weeded and watered the plants.

Millie knew that since Papa was a pastor, he had to work hard and didn't have time for tending gardens. Mamma said that many people depended upon Papa. And it was true. Some nights the telephone would ring while everyone was asleep, and Papa would get up to answer it. After hanging up, he would dress and go out in the cold, dark night. Sometimes it was to visit a family who had lost a son in the terrible war. And Papa would return exhausted, with his shoulders slumped. But he always said the Lord was faithful and would give him strength for what he must do.

After the vegetable canning was completed, Millie and Benjamin went to town with Mamma again. This time they went to the shoe store. During summer Millie and Benjamin usually went barefoot, but with school starting they needed shoes. Mamma said Benjamin's feet had grown "like yeast bread." Millie's feet were a size bigger, too. Millie knew they didn't have much money for shoes, but Mamma always said, "God takes good care of us. Somehow He always provides for our needs, and we must be thankful." Millie was thankful. She loved new shoes. She smoothed her hand over her shiny brown oxfords. She would not wear these new shoes until the very first day of school.

After buying shoes, they purchased pencils and erasers at the five-and-ten-cent store. Since Millie and Benjamin had been such good helpers with the canning, Papa said they could each get a new paper tablet. Millie was so happy! More than

anything, she loved to draw. Both sides of every page in her old paper tablet were used up, but now she would have fresh pages. Someday she hoped to get a set of colored pencils, but for now, she must be content with plain lead pencils. Papa often said, "Count your blessings one by one." And Millie counted any kind of pencil as a good blessing.

Then one day an exciting package wrapped in brown paper arrived from the catalog store. Most of the contents were for Benjamin, since Mamma was sewing for Millie. There were corduroy pants and plaid flannel shirts, but everything was just a little too big. "That's fine," Mamma said. "Benjamin's growing like a beanstalk." Then, at the bottom of the box, Millie discovered blue snow pants and a

matching blue-and-red jacket for herself. "I can hardly wait for the snow!" she exclaimed as she pulled on her new snow pants. "Do you think it'll snow early this year, Mamma?"

Finally school was only a day away! Millie stood before her open bedroom window and felt the cool breeze on her face. Fall was in the air! She looked down at the pathway that wound from the house up the hill. That was how they got to school until cold weather set in and forced them to ride the school bus. It was a long walk, but Millie enjoyed every step. She liked calling "hello" to old Widow Long, who sat on her porch in a wicker rocker having a "morning breath of fresh air." Sometimes she would climb up on Farmer Powell's fence and listen to his goats bleat a noisy "good-morning." Farmer Powell also had five grown sons and a younger daughter, Katy, who was Millie's favorite baby-sitter. Katy often stayed at the parsonage when Papa and Mamma went out of town to a conference. And often when Katy was there, her brother Robert Wesley would stop in too. Millie and Benjamin loved Robert Wesley like an older brother. He told wonderful stories and liked to play games with them.

That evening before bed, Millie carefully laid out her new blue jumper on the chair. And one by one she tucked her new pencils and erasers and tablet into her bag. Then she lay in bed thinking about tomorrow. She would walk to school with Benjamin. Mamma would wave good-bye from the front door. Old Widow Long would smile from her rocker on the porch. Millie snuggled down under her bedcovers. She couldn't wait for morning! She listened to the sparrows' good-night songs as darkness fell. Millie wondered how she could possibly sleep. Tomorrow was the first day of a brand-new school year!

Chapter 2

MILLIE'S DISAPPOINTMENT

The next morning Millie awoke with a dull pain drumming in her head. She pressed her hands against her ears and shut her eyes tight, hoping to squeeze away the hurt. But it was no use. Tossing back her covers, she pulled herself up. The usually pleasant smell of bacon and eggs turned her stomach. Eyeing the blue jumper neatly laid upon the chair and her new shoes beneath, all Millie could think of was the horrible pounding in her head.

From the bottom of the stairs, Papa cheerfully called, "Millie, Benjamin, it's time that all good people were rising! Mamma has a fine breakfast cooking. Dress yourselves, and mind you, don't dilly-dally. You don't want to be late for the first day of school."

Millie heard a thud as Benjamin's feet hit the hardwood floor. A moment later he poked his head through Millie's doorway and exclaimed,

"Hey, don't just sit there! You'd better get dressed, Millie. Have you forgotten? Vacation time is over and we have to go back to school today."

A shiver passed through Millie and all at once she felt both hot and cold. Hot tears of disappointment began to trickle down her cheeks. Millie had looked forward to this day for such a long time. There was nothing as wonderful as the first day of school, and now Millie felt certain she would miss it.

"Benjamin, I don't feel good," sobbed Millie. Benjamin walked over to her bed. Frowning, he looked more closely.

"That's too bad, Millie. You don't look very good. I'll get Mamma. She'll take care of you. And don't cry, Millie—school's not that important! I wish I could stay home, even for one more day!"

Benjamin ran down the stairs calling to Mamma. Millie's head felt like it was spinning

around and around in a dizzy circle. Suddenly she felt cold. She curled into a ball underneath her covers, and her teeth began to chatter. Her head throbbed even worse than before.

Mamma looked concerned as she walked into Millie's bedroom and laid a comforting hand on Millie's forehead. "Oh dear, Millicent Ruth, you feel like you've been in the oven with the biscuits I baked for breakfast! You certainly have a fever. You must be a sick girl."

Millie began to cry again, partly in relief, for she knew Mamma would take good care of her. Mamma always knew just what to do. Millie told Mamma about the pain in her head. She continued to shiver and shake, and Mamma explained how a fever can make a person feel both hot and cold at the same time. She understood how miserable Millie felt.

"You'll soon feel fine again—all well and ready for school. But today we'll keep you in bed. It won't be long until you'll be in school with all the other children!" Mamma handed Millie a glass of water and asked her to take a good drink. "Swallow this pill, Millie dear. It will help take away that fever. You

go back to sleep now. When you wake up you'll probably feel much better." Mamma gave Millie a kiss and tucked an extra blanket around her.

Even though she still felt horrible, Millie was comforted and secure in Mamma's loving care. She soon slid off into a restless sleep. Her dreams were confused with funny little men running in and out of her head pounding away with huge black hammers on what appeared to be tall trees or narrow bones.

When Millie awoke, the room was bathed in a yellow glow from the muted sun that shone behind the closed window blinds. Mamma said the hurt would soon be gone, but it certainly hadn't left yet! Millie pressed her hands against her temples. They felt hot—very, very hot! She wished the "soon" that Mamma had talked about would hurry up.

The house was quiet. Since it was Monday, Mamma was perhaps in the basement working on the wash. Loneliness washed over Millie as she remembered that today was the first day of school. Her friends were in the classroom right that moment getting new books and sharing stories of summer adventures. At recess there would be hopscotch, jump rope, swings, and breathless games of tag. The pounding in her head reminded Millie of why she was at home instead of with all her friends. Suddenly she felt so miserable that she was quite content to snuggle down in the comfort of her bed.

Just as Millie began to wish for Mamma's company, a knock sounded at the front door. She heard voices but couldn't tell who it was, and felt too wretched to care. Then footsteps sounded on the stairs and she heard Mamma say, "She's been sleeping most of the day, which I suppose is good. I am, however, disturbed over her high fever. I'm thankful you came, Dr. Neils."

So it was the family doctor. Millie liked big Dr. Neils. Because he was an older man, he had not gone off to the war to care for wounded soldiers. Still, he stood tall and straight with broad shoulders, and looked more like a football player than a doctor. Millie often thought that his pleasant, jovial manner did as much good as the medicine he gave.

Entering the bedroom, Dr. Neils raised his bushy gray eyebrows and gave Millie a wink and a mischievous grin. "Now, now, Millie girl, this is a fine set of circumstances. Look at you, here in bed on the first day of school. My, my, we can't have that kind of behavior from someone as bright as my Millie girl! Let's take a look at you. What seems to be the problem?"

Dr. Neils listened intently as Millie described the dull pounding in her head and the chills that left her cold and hot at the same time. He nodded his head and squinted his eyes as he always did when he was concentrating. His large, gentle hands examined Millie's head. When he touched a tender area behind her left ear, Millie winced from the pain. Dr. Neils nodded again, then peered down Millie's throat with his funny little flashlight. He looked into her eyes and nose, and then with another small instrument that felt cold but didn't hurt, he examined her ears.

"Millie, I want you to take this medicine that I'm leaving with your mother. We'll have to wait and see if it helps you. I believe the pain will go away and you'll feel better soon. We certainly must get you back on your feet so you can go to school!" said Dr. Neils.

He gave Millie an affectionate pat on the shoulder, then turned to leave. As the doctor went down the stairs Millie overheard him say, "Millie has a serious infection in the mastoid bone behind her ear. I hope it doesn't go into her brain and develop into encephalitis. We'll keep a close watch on her." Millie had never heard those funny words before, but right now her head hurt too much to care.

Later that afternoon Millie began to feel a little better. Mamma propped her up in bed with several big pillows and opened the window blinds so Millie could look outside. She could see Widow Long's house and a portion of her wide front porch where the old widow sat in her rocking chair. If Millie  listened really hard, she could hear the squeaking of the chair as the widow rocked back and forth.

Millie had often wondered about Widow Long. She was all alone and seldom did any visiting. Sometimes Millie and Benjamin could get her to tell them tales of her childhood long ago. Once she began talking, she would lose herself in her stories and ramble on and on. Millie had heard that Widow Long was very wealthy, but she wondered what the old lady did with her money. She seemed to spend most of her time rocking in her chair, feeding her cats, or walking slowly through her rose garden.

Suddenly Millie noticed Benjamin walking down the pathway toward home. He paused for a moment in front of the widow's porch. When Widow Long beckoned to him, he walked up her steps and began to chat. Benjamin was no doubt telling all about his first day at school. Millie envied him. If only she could be there with them! Now Widow Long would probably talk about her school days.

Millie slid back down under her covers pouting and feeling sorry for herself. After all, was it really fair that she, who loved school so dearly, had gotten sick right on the first day of the new school year? And that Benjamin, who never enjoyed school, felt fine and had gone to school that first day? Millie struggled to hold back her tears. Then, feeling the dizzying pain in her ear, Millie's shoulders shook as she sobbed into her pillow, wishing fervently that the first day of school had never happened.

Chapter 3

A FRIEND SAYS GOOD-BYE

Morning after morning, Millie watched from her bedroom window as Benjamin walked off to school. His books, held together by one of Papa's old belts, were always slung over his shoulder. Before going up the hill he would turn around and wave good-bye to Millie. Even though she knew Benjamin could not see her sitting propped up against her pillows, Millie waved a little good-bye in his direction. Then she would think, "Tomorrow— maybe tomorrow I'll be well enough to go to school." But tomorrow always found Millie too sick to get out of bed.

It seemed like ages since that first day of school. Millie took pleasure in watching through her window as the leaves fluttered down through autumn breezes in a beautiful array of colors. Evenings brought the scent of bonfires and cool, swirling mists as the sun sank low in the sky. The days grew shorter until it was no longer light outside at bedtime. Millie never could quite understand why in the summer months she had to go to bed when it was still light outside. God's world was a funny one! Still, Papa often said how thankful they should be for the world that God had designed in such an orderly fashion.

It wouldn't be long before the first snowfall. Certainly by then the horrible, pounding ache in Millie's head would go away and she could join the other children at school. Now when Dr. Neils came to visit he wore his warm wool suit and his heavy tweed overcoat. He would rub his big hands together vigorously to warm them up. Regardless of the cold weather or his long, tiring hours of work, Dr. Neils always spoke cheerfully to Millie.

"Somehow this infection hasn't left you yet," Dr. Neils said as he examined Millie's ear. "You're a good girl, and you are such a patient girl. I know it's not fun being sick for such a long time. I'll have to call you my patient little patient!"

Millie giggled but hoped she would not have to be a patient patient much longer.

One November evening friends from church gathered in Millie's home for prayer meeting. Because of the war, it cost a lot of money to buy coal for the church. To help out, every family in the church took a turn having prayer meeting at their home. Even Papa studied for his sermons in his little study at home instead of working in the church office.

The doorbell began to ring and Millie heard friendly voices as people arrived. Millie couldn't hear their conversations very well, but she could hear the songs they sang as the meeting began. How she loved hearing the sweet music that told of God's love and care! She could just picture Papa rocking up and down on his

heels as he always did when he led the singing. And every once in a while she could hear Farmer Powell's shrill tenor voice screeching above the other voices. Sometimes his singing made her think of fingernails scratching on a blackboard, but she loved Farmer Powell and that helped her overlook his singing. Millie thought that everyone else ignored his singing for the same reason.

When the singing stopped, Millie heard someone begin to pray. She wished she could be downstairs with the others. In the hallway Benjamin was stretched out on his stomach in his baggy flannel pajamas. He poked his head between the banister spindles and peered intently down into the living room. "Old Widow Long is praying," he reported in a loud whisper. Benjamin was supposed to be in bed. Then Millie heard a soft footstep on the stairway. She almost laughed out loud as Benjamin jumped to his feet and hurried off in the direction of his bedroom. Then he paused by her door to whisper, "It's Robert Wesley!"

Millie and Benjamin loved Robert Wesley! He always seemed to bubble over with fun and laughter. Tall and handsome, he was the best big brother anyone could wish for. Benjamin grabbed Robert Wesley's hand and pulled him into Millie's room, then quietly shut the door. It was a delicious feeling to have Robert Wesley for a visit! The vicious pain that so often plagued Millie instantly faded to a nagging ache.

"Well now, Millie, my favorite girl, I just had to come upstairs to say good-night to you and Ben." Robert Wesley always shortened Benjamin to Ben, which of course made Benjamin feel almost as grown-up as Robert Wesley himself.

Millie loved Robert Wesley's funny stories. But even more than his stories, Millie loved to sit by Robert Wesley's side as he played his mountain dulcimer. When his fingers ran across the strings of the long, graceful instrument, the music was so sweet that it made Millie think of heaven.

Since he hadn't brought his dulcimer, Robert Wesley entertained the children with funny stories. They giggled as he reminded them of how the old, cranky gander chased Millie as she ran after fireflies in the farmyard. Then he let them in on a secret prank. A certain older lady, who always sat near the back of the church, liked to slip her shoes off during the sermon. One Sunday when Robert Wesley served as an usher, he had secretly taken one of her shoes and set it right in the middle of the foyer! The children laughed till they cried as Robert Wesley described the woman's surprised face when she discovered that her shoe had strayed.

Checking his watch, Robert Wesley said, "Now look how late it is! Prayer meeting must be almost over, and if your mamma catches me up here keeping you two awake, she'll never send me any of her good cookies while I'm away."

"Away? Where are you going?" Millie and Benjamin asked in unison.

"Oh, I almost forgot to tell you! I've signed up for the army, and I have to leave soon to go into training. I need to learn how to become a good soldier. Then I'll be able to do my part to protect our country and maybe help bring this ugly old war to an end."

All his brothers had already gone off to war, but Millie and Benjamin never thought that Robert Wesley would go away too. Millie knew that going to war was a serious thing. She reached out for Robert Wesley's hand as big tears rolled down her cheeks. To her surprise, Benjamin was crying too. Robert Wesley put his strong arms around both children.

"Say now, you both must be brave. I'll miss you very much, but I'll be home for a visit at Christmas. I have an idea—I'll write letters to you, especially if you'll write back to me. Now, how about a smile from each of you?"

Robert Wesley grinned in his own special way. Millie and Benjamin nodded their heads in agreement, but it was hard to smile.

"And Millie, I want you to be all well by Christmastime!" added Robert Wesley firmly.

Millie wanted to say, "I'll try," but she couldn't get the words out over the lump in her throat. Robert Wesley bent down and kissed her forehead and said good-bye.

Downstairs the church people were singing "I've Found a Friend." It was one of Millie's favorite songs. It was a happy song about Jesus. Jesus was Millie's most beloved friend, but as the familiar tune drifted up to Millie's room, she could only think of her good friend Robert Wesley, who would soon be far away. She turned her head toward the window. Through the darkness the lamppost shone its light along a pathway of silently falling snow. The first snow was falling at last and it looked very cold.

Chapter 4

HAPPINESS IN HIDDEN PLACES

After Robert Wesley and the rest of the church friends left, the house seemed cold and quiet. Millie's pounding head and worried heart kept her awake far into the night. When her fever rose, Mamma gave her another dose of Dr. Neils's medicine. Finally the fever and pain subsided and she fell into a fitful sleep.

When Millie awoke, the sun barely peeked through gray clouds. The scattered autumn leaves were now hidden beneath a thick layer of newly fallen snow. Birds flew in flustered groups, circling around and over the tree branches that were bent low under the snow that covered them like fluffy swirls of whipped cream.

Millie sensed Benjamin's excitement as she heard him quickly dress. When he stomped noisily down the stairs Papa called out, "Benjamin, Benjamin! Please quiet down! Millie had a restless night and she needs extra sleep this morning!"

Usually Millie was excited by the first snow of the season. But she felt no joy today. This would be just one more thing to miss. She looked out the window and saw Benjamin playing in the knee-deep snow. Soon the bus came, leaving crunchy grooves in the snow as it moved up the hill past Widow Long's house.

Now Widow Long would sit inside rather than on her front porch. Millie could see a dim light glowing in the widow's front window where one of her calico cats sat rubbing its head against the wooden frame.

After bringing Millie a breakfast of piping-hot oatmeal and toast, Mamma set up her ironing board beside Millie's bed. The freshly washed pile of clothing was stacked high above the rim of the big wicker laundry basket. "It looks like I'll be up

here with you most of the day," Mamma said with a smile.

"Good!" Millie responded. Having Mamma close by meant that she wouldn't be so lonely. "Will you tell me stories about when you were a little girl?"

Millie listened as Mamma spoke of happy times long ago. Before Millie knew it, the clothes had disappeared from the basket and were hanging in a neat row on the hook over the door. As Mamma took down the ironing board she said, "Millie, we need to be thankful for each day God gives us. God always tucks happiness in hidden places. It's up to us to look for those places and discover the delightful bits of happiness He has placed there." Millie knew that Mamma understood how hard it was for her to be content lying in bed when the snow outside looked so inviting.

A slam of the door signaled Benjamin's return from school. He jerked off his wet boots and snow pants, ran up the stairs, and burst into Millie's room like a gust of wind.

"Guess what, Millie! You're going to have company!" Benjamin cried.

"Who, Benjamin? Please tell me," Millie pleaded.

Benjamin plopped himself down on the end of Millie's bed. "It's Anna Sue. She told me in school today how she wishes you'd hurry up and get well. She misses you awfully much. Anyway, she wants to come see you. Is it okay, Mamma?"

Benjamin and Millie both looked in Mamma's direction and waited anxiously for her answer. Mamma thought a minute and said, "I suppose there's no harm in having her here for a bit. Anna Sue is a thoughtful friend, but I don't want you to get tired, Millie."

Then Papa arrived and joined in the discussion. "A fire in the fireplace is just the thing for our first snow. Millie, how would you like it if I carried you down to the living room for Anna Sue's visit?"

Millie clapped her hands with joy as Papa bundled her in a big blanket and carried her downstairs. It had been so long since she had been downstairs that somehow everything looked a little different. Still, it most certainly was home. With a bright, warm fire crackling in the old stone fireplace and the family sitting together, Millie felt happier than she had in a long time.

When the doorbell rang, pretty red-cheeked Anna Sue came in with snowflakes clinging to her curls and a cheerful smile on her face. In that moment Millie just knew that somehow, someday she would be well again.

After friendly greetings, Anna Sue exclaimed, "Look, Millie! Look here at what was sitting on your doorstep. It's all wrapped up and it has your name on it!"

Millie looked at the box and asked, "Is it from you, Anna Sue?"

"No—I just found it on the stairs. Honest!"

Anna Sue set the box on Millie's lap, and Papa looked at the tag. "It's strange," he said. "Millie's name is on it, but there's no return address or indication of who sent it."

"Open it, Millie!" Benjamin urged. "Maybe something inside will tell who gave it to you."

Benjamin helped Millie remove the string and wrapping paper. Inside they found a sturdy but delicately designed tin box with a tight-fitting lid. It was decorated with beautiful little flowers and butterflies of blue, lavender, pink, and green.

"Take the lid off, Millie!" implored Benjamin, unable to control his curiosity.

"But wait, Millie dear—look, there is a note taped to the lid. Perhaps you should read it before you look inside," Mamma suggested.

"Mamma's right, Millie. See what it says," Papa agreed. Millie pulled off the small envelope. Her full name was printed on it with bright red ink.

"It says, 'To Millicent Ruth,'" announced Millie. "Hmm...it's from someone who knows my whole name." Then Millie read the note out loud. "'From within this box of sunshine, each gift opened at a special time will give friendship, fun, happiness, life, strength, and love. All of this is given to you from this box of sunshine.'"

Millie looked puzzled; Papa frowned; Mamma shook her head; Anna Sue shrugged her shoulders; and Benjamin said, "Does it really matter who gave it to you, Millie? Come on—take the lid off!"

For what seemed to be a very long moment, the whole room hung in silence. Only the cheerful crackling of the fire could be heard as Millie stared at the box in her lap. Then she looked over at Mamma and said, "Remember what you told me about how God tucks away some happiness in each day?" Mamma smiled and nodded. Suddenly Millie's hands went to work tugging at the edge of the tin lid, working it up farther and farther until with one noisy pop, the lid was off.

Chapter 5

THE MYSTERIOUS BOX

Millie peered into the golden depths of the Sunshine Box with breathless delight. Her eyes lit up as she discovered an array of unknown objects of various sizes, wrapped in filmy tissue paper in a rainbow of colors and each one tied in a golden bow that glittered and sparkled in the dancing light from the fireplace.

"Oh—just look! Oh—just look!" was all she could manage to say. Millie almost felt that to do more than just look would spoil this moment of happiness that God had tucked into her day—that it might vanish and be gone forever. But no, it was a gift. A whole box of gifts! And gifts were to be opened and enjoyed.

So one by one, Millie lifted out the gifts ever so carefully. There were six altogether. Just as the note indicated, a small white tag was attached to the gold bow on each gift. The tags contained instructions explaining when Millie should unwrap each one. One tag said, "Open on an especially happy day," while another tag said, "Be sure to open this gift in the springtime."

How strange and mysterious, but how delightfully wonderful! Millie continued to examine the contents of the box until she discovered something special about the very small gift wrapped in bright red paper. She read the tag out loud: "'Please open me up right away!'" Millie laughed. Benjamin, Anna Sue, Mamma, and Papa all watched with excitement. Delighted that she would soon see what was inside the gift, Millie untied the bow and tore off the wrapping as fast as her hands could manage. Then she stared in wonder at the first gift.

"Look, it's a bird, Mamma—a little, bitty bird with pretty wings and feathers. And look at its yellow bill!" Mamma had always loved birds. She and Millie enjoyed watching the sparrows that gathered each morning to nibble at the dry bread crumbs Mamma scattered on Millie's windowsill.

"My goodness," Mamma exclaimed, "isn't it a lovely little bird, Millie! Why, it's all but perfect!"

"But it's not real—not really a real bird, is it? Look. It doesn't move—not even a little bit," Anna Sue observed.

"Of course it's not real!" Benjamin retorted. "It would fly away if it were really alive. Just the same, it sure does look like a real bird!"

Papa looked down at Millie, who had become rather quiet. He ruffled her blonde hair and asked softly, "What do you think, Millie? It's your gift...."

Millie looked long and hard, up and down and all around the small bird from the top of its soft downy head to the tip of its turned-up tail feathers. Its two funny legs were just slightly larger than toothpicks, and it sat on mustard-colored, clawed feet.

"I don't care if it isn't real. It doesn't matter to me. He's mine and I love him. He'll always be mine and I'll always love him! And tomorrow if my head hurts, I can look at him and remember how

happy I felt today!" Mamma and Papa gave Millie sad little smiles. The excitement had taken its toll on Millie. Her head drooped and her eyelids felt heavy. Anna Sue whispered a soft "good-bye" and tiptoed out of the house.

Millie heard Mamma say, "A merry heart does good like a medicine." Then Mamma gently lifted the small "almost real" bird from Millie's lap and placed it on the marble-topped coffee table. She left the lid off the Sunshine Box so Millie could enjoy one last look inside before Papa carried her back up to her bedroom. Millie didn't know when she would feel well again; but for the present moment, her heart felt merry, and the mysterious Sunshine Box had indeed been the very best medicine!

Chapter 6

AN AMAZING NEW FRIEND

When Papa carried Millie upstairs and tucked her in, Mamma placed the Sunshine Box and the little bird on the bedside table. Millie gazed at the beautiful gift in wonder until finally her eyelids drooped and she drifted off to sleep.

In the middle of the night a fierce wind began to race and whirl around the corners of the house. Millie suddenly awoke. She snuggled down between her feather mattress and a layer of padded quilts and listened to the howling wind. But it wasn't the wind that had roused her. Nor was it the banging of the loose shutter outside her window. It was something else—a small sound with a high, squeaky pitch. It was a sad sound, like a wee child crying over a lost toy.

Millie lay there staring into the darkness, not daring to move a muscle. The pain was still behind her ear and inside her head. She listened intently

again for the sound, but all she heard was the storm outside. "Silly Millie—you must have dreamed it," she thought. Then, just as she rolled over to go back to sleep, the sound came again. This time it was clear and precise, streaking sharply through the air like lightning on a warm summer night. It was there as fast as it was gone—but it was there! And within a single heartbeat it was there again! Millie didn't know if she should feel curious or scared. But there it was again! Certainly there was no mistaking that sound. It was the small but sharp peep of a bird!

The birds that ate bread crumbs from the windowsill had been gone since yesterday morning. Millie had watched them flit about, devouring the shared morsels left over from the family's breakfast. During the day Millie had seen an occasional bird hopping across the limbs of the

nearby trees, but with the sky graying and an approaching snowstorm once more in the air, the feathered creatures had flown off to their various places of shelter.

Now, here in the middle of this stormy night, Millie was certain she had heard a bird, and yet how was that possible? She reached over to her bedside table and turned on the lamp. As Millie's eyes grew accustomed to the lamp's yellow glow, she sat up. She pulled her covers up to her chin and peered around the room. Millie looked far into the corners, crouched down low to see beneath her dresser, then craned her neck to see the knick-knack shelf that hung on the wall nearest her bed. Maybe her bookcase was hiding something, but it was so full of her favorite books that there hardly seemed room for a bird.

There it was again! With a startled jump, Millie caught her breath. She turned her head toward the sound. Right there on her bedside table, sitting beneath her lamp, was the little toy bird. Her own bird from the Sunshine Box that had looked "almost real" right from the moment she unwrapped it. But now its head slowly turned and its small round eyes looked straight into Millie's. She couldn't believe it! The bird was real—the bird from her Sunshine Box was unbelievably, unmistakably, without a doubt, really alive!

Millie shook her head and said in a hushed whisper, "You're real! You're not a little toy bird. You're alive!" The bird nodded its small head and let out another crooked-sounding peep. Millie sat and stared, trying to understand how this could be. "I still can't understand—I mean, how can you be a real bird and not just a toy bird? But I'm glad! Oh, I'm so glad you're alive. So hello, Little Bitty Bird!"

Then something else new and strange happened. The little bird opened its yellow bill and said quite clearly, "I'm glad you're alive too! So hello, big Millie girl!"

Millie giggled with delight. "I thought you could only peep. Did I really understand what you just said to me?"

"Oh, peep, yes, I can use people talk or I can use bird talk. Right now, whichever way I talk, it doesn't help me feel happy. I'm afraid I may never be happy again!" The bird's head drooped sadly.

"But why do you say that? You are such a clever bird. How can you possibly be unhappy?"

"Oh, that's simple. You see, I was put in the Sunshine Box to make you happy, but then because I am such a selfish bird, I forgot all about your happiness and began thinking of my own! You see, I'm so tired of being just a toy bird. I want to be like those birds that gather on your window-sill every morning!" The bird sighed. "If I were only with them, flying merrily through the sky, then I would truly be happy!"

Millie thought a moment; she certainly did not want this small gift of hers to be unhappy. Suddenly her face brightened. "I have an idea. I'll open my window for you and set you free! You see, I understand how you feel. I hate being sick. I want to get well so I can go to school and be with my friends. I want to wear my new snowsuit and play with my sled. I'd love to visit Widow Long again, and go back to church, and play with my friend, Anna Sue. I hate being sick and want so badly to be well! So you see, we're alike! You want to be like the other birds and I want to be like the other children."

Little Bitty Bird cocked his head and asked, "Would you really open your window and let me go? Oh, that would be so wonderful. I would be free! How could I ever thank you?" He stopped abruptly, then continued. "No, that would not be good. I'm your gift. I'm supposed to bring happiness. If I leave I can't make you happy." He paused. "But on the other hand, if I only left once in a while, and if I always came back, then we could both be happy!"

"That sounds fine to me," Millie replied.

"Maybe I can even take you with me some-times, Millie, if you would like that," suggested the bird. Millie laughed at the idea. Of course she didn't know how to fly.

As if understanding her thoughts, the bird said, "It could be done. You need to simply shrink down to my size, climb on my back, sit quietly in my feathers, and off we'd go. It'd be such fun! A change would be good for you, and then I'd be like other birds." Millie sank into her pillow. This was too much to take in. Was she really awake, or was this just a dream? Little Bitty Bird hopped across her table, flew over the lamp, and landed on her shoulder. He leaned forward and whispered, "Come with me, Millie! It's very simple. Think hard. The harder you think the smaller you'll become. Then off we'll go! But before you shrink, you must open the window."

Millie thought some more. After pulling on her bathrobe, she reached over from her bed and opened the window. Then suddenly she felt herself shrinking. Indeed, she became extremely small! Millie jumped quickly on top of Little Bitty Bird. The next thing she knew, she and the bird flew right out through the open window!

Oh, what fun! What sheer joy it was to soar through the night with the snow blowing gently in circles around them! Millie nestled down in Little Bitty Bird's soft, warm feathers. The wind grew calm as the moon crept from behind a cloud. Up and down they flew over white-topped hills dotted with trees of silver. On and on they went over snow-covered rooftops and through swirls of smoke rising from sturdy stone chimneys.

"It's wonderful, Little Bitty Bird!" Millie cried.

"It's fantastic! You have made me so happy!" The bird responded with happy peeps that sounded very much like a song. But as they continued, the wind rose once more and thick clouds blocked the moon. Suddenly the two small travelers felt fearful and confused. Little Bitty Bird flapped his wings hard against the stinging winter wind. "Peep, peep, peep!" the poor bird cried. The journey was no longer wonderful. Snow was falling heavily now, and Millie could not see the light from her window.

"Please take me home now, Little Bitty Bird. I'm getting scared! It isn't fun anymore," Millie cried.

"It's not fun for me either. But I don't know how to find the way back. I'm afraid we're lost!" peeped the frightened bird.

Millie raised her voice against the wind. "Papa always says that God will take care of us. He'll help us—I know He will. But maybe we should have stayed home..."

It was then that a thin, silvery voice whispered on the wind. "God will take care of you through night or day and all the way," said the voice. "God will take care of you, God will take care of you."

"Follow that voice!" Millie cried. "It's from God, I know! I think God has sent an angel to guide us!"

Little Bitty Bird listened hard. He followed the voice, bravely beating his wings against the freezing wind. At last they were home! The voice brought them right to Millie's window. Through the open window they flew. The bird flopped in an exhausted heap on the corner of Millie's bed. As she tumbled off his back, she instantly grew to her normal size. Her head dropped into her pillow. What a relief to be home! She blinked her eyes and wondered over her amazing adventure. How thankful she was that God had sent an angel to bring them home. Millie fell into a deep, dreamless sleep.

The next morning, Millie awoke with a smile on her face. Just then, Mamma walked in with a breakfast tray, and before she could even set it down, Millie poured out her amazing story.

"Mamma, something so wonderful happened last night—I hardly know where to begin! My little bird from the Sunshine Box is not just a toy bird at all! First I heard him peeping, and then he talked to me. He told me how to make myself small, and then we flew out the window! You can't imagine what it feels like to fly, Mamma. But then the storm got worse and Little Bitty Bird could hardly fly. And then we were lost! But God sent an angel to guide us home." Mamma appeared puzzled. "You do believe me, don't you, Mamma?" Millie asked.

Mamma thought a moment, then replied, "Millicent Ruth, you had such a difficult night. Your fever went up quite high. Papa and I stayed by your bedside most of the night. I imagine, dear, that you were just dreaming."

"Oh no, Mamma, I could not have been dreaming. It was all real—so very real! I do remember feeling warm, even hot, but when my little bird took me out into the snowy sky, it felt just wonderful!"

"Well, dear, it's of no matter now. You eat your breakfast and then you can tell me more about your adventure. It does sound exciting!" Mamma laid the tray on Millie's lap, then patted her shoulder. "Dr. Neils will be stopping in later today. You'll have to remember to show him your little bird from the Sunshine Box."

Millie looked out her window as she nibbled on her toast and jelly. The sun was shining and the sky was one vast expanse of intense blue. The snow almost danced with sparkles of bright merriment. Just as she finished her hot cereal, a familiar "Peep, peep, peep!" caught her attention.

She looked at the little bird on her bedside table. His head was cocked to one side, and he winked one of his round eyes, as if to say, "You and I know it's all true, don't we! We did fly into the night together."

Millie nodded her head. She knew the little bird was more than a toy—he was her friend and he was alive! "Thanks, Little Bitty Bird, for all of last night. It was such fun! And I'm so glad God helped us and showed us the way home."

The little bird nodded. "It was fun, Millie, but we'll have to wait until the right time before we take another journey."

"That's all right. I understand. Besides, we can still be good friends right here in my bedroom." The bird stood very still, with his head of brown fluff cocked at an angle where he could watch both his new friend and the birds who  would soon gather on the windowsill for their morning feast of crumbs. Millie smiled to herself. She was thankful to have Little Bitty Bird for her special friend.

Chapter 7

THE OPERATION

*P*apa walked into Millie's room and bent down to give her a kiss on the cheek. "Good morning, honey girl," he said in a gentle voice.

"Papa, I love you and Mamma," declared Millie. "Mamma said you both stayed with me most all of last night. I can't remember it, but I'm glad you were here. Are you very tired, Papa?"

"I'm fine. And besides, it was worth it just to see how much better you look now. I'm glad you trusted God to guide you safely back from your adventure. It's true what the voice told you—God will take care of you, through night or day, and all the way, God will take care of you. And Millie, the Bible tells us that God never forgets to take care of the little sparrow birds. And did you know that it also says that you are far more valuable to God than a whole flock of sparrows? So certainly, God is caring for you. You're going to be well again, but we do need to be patient. And I believe that God will send us plenty of happiness during these hard times!"

"Oh Papa, I am happy! I have a new friend," Millie remarked as she pointed to the little bird (who now looked very much like a toy bird) perched on her bedside table.

Papa listened quietly as Millie related what had happened during the night. He smiled and said he understood. Whether she had been dreaming or pretending, Papa was thankful for Millie's happiness.

"Millie, no matter how long it takes for you to get well and strong again, we do so want you to be happy. You'll need to be very brave, for I know you don't feel well and at times your ear and head really hurt."

"I'll try, Papa," Millie answered solemnly.

Then, with a twinkle in his eye, Papa said, "Maybe we should take a peek into the Sunshine Box. There might be a gift for this very day!" He carried the beautiful box over to Millie's bed and took off the lid. Together they searched through the five remaining gifts until they found a long narrow box wrapped in beautiful blue tissue paper. Its tag said, "For the first morning of the second snowfall."

"Papa, that's today! Last night it snowed. It was our second snowstorm. Please, let's do open it right away!"

Papa nodded, and Millie carefully opened the gift. It felt very light and fragile. Millie frowned as she first looked at the new gift in its thin white box.

"It's a feather! This is a strange gift! But it is pretty, isn't it, Papa? Look, it's so blue."

"Yes, Millie, and look how many shades of blue you can see when the sunlight touches it," Papa said. "Why, I believe it's a beautiful gift! Someday when you get those colored pencils you want so badly, you must draw a picture of this lovely feather."

"You're right, Papa, I will! Where should I put it for now? Maybe I could put it some-place where I can see it all the time."

Just then Mamma and Dr. Neils entered the room. Millie told Dr. Neils all about the Sunshine Box. She showed him her bird and then showed both Dr. Neils and Mamma her beautiful blue feather.

"Well, Millie girl, I'm happy for you," said the kindly doctor. "And I'm glad to see the happy roses in your cheeks after your adventuresome night!"

Mamma picked up the feather and said, "How about putting your feather in a small flower vase? We can put it here on your bedside table next to your little bird, Millie."

After Dr. Neils examined Millie, he patted her cheek and said, "I think it's time you visited the hospital, Millie. While you're there, I'll operate on that place behind your ear where it hurts. You'll be asleep and you won't feel any pain at all. I'll work very carefully to take out the infection that makes your head hurt so badly. And then, before you know it you'll be home again. What do you think of that?"

Millie shook her head. "But today I feel better. Why do I have to go to the hospital now? I really am better!" she cried.

"Millie dear," Mamma said, "we all love you and we want your suffering to end. Some days you do feel better, but the infection is still there. We only want what is best."

"Besides that, Millie," Dr. Neils added, "your Mamma or Papa will be able to stay with you. You'll sleep a lot and soon your pain will be all gone."

Little Bitty Bird gave Millie a little wink. Millie fought back tears trying to conceal her apprehension. She knew Mamma was right and that Dr. Neils would take good care of her. Everything would be fine—it just had to be. Papa patted Millie lovingly on her shoulder and gave

her a quiet reminder of God's promise of care— the promise she had heard during the trip in the night with Little Bitty Bird. Above all else, Millie knew she must not forget that promise. Everything would be fine—it just had to be.

Just as Mamma had said, Dr. Neils took good care of her in the hospital. And even as the nurse prepared her for surgery, Millie thought about God's promise to care for her.

When Millie finally opened her eyes the next day she saw the nurse standing beside her in a crisp white uniform. She felt the nurse's soft hand smooth back her hair. Millie still felt drowsy. It wouldn't be hard to go back to sleep again, but her curiosity kept her awake for the present time.

"Good morning, Millie. My, but you have been quite the sleepyhead!"

"Where's Mamma?" Millie asked, feeling as though the sound of her own voice came from somewhere far away.

"Your mother just stepped out for a cup of tea. She'll be back shortly. I told her I'd stay with you until she returned. How do you feel, Millie?"

"A little strange," Millie answered. Her head was sore, especially behind her left ear, but it was not extremely painful. She reached back and touched her bandages.

Now she remembered. It seemed like it had happened only a few minutes ago. Papa and Mamma had dressed her in her snowsuit and driven her to the hospital. Getting out of the house had been fun, but tiring. When they reached the hospital Millie was relieved to crawl into the fresh-smelling, smoothly starched sheets of the high-standing hospital bed. From the window in her hospital room Millie could see the town below with all the shops and people busily walking from one place to another. It felt very different from the view she was used to seeing from her bedroom window at home.

Millie felt comfortable in her new surroundings. The doctors and nurses were friendly and kind. Dr. Neils stopped in that evening to explain exactly what would happen the next morning.

Mamma stayed all that evening until Millie fell asleep. And Mamma was there when Millie awoke the

next morning. Had she been sitting there all night? Millie didn't quite know. After taking a pill the nurse gave her, Millie felt very sleepy. She soon drifted off into a strange emptiness. She could only vaguely recall hearing voices once in a while, Mamma's hand holding hers, and then nothing—nothing at all until now.

"Is it all over? I mean, the operation—is it all finished?" Millie asked the nurse.

"Oh goodness, yes! Your operation was yesterday. You've been such a good girl and you've certainly been sleeping a lot, which of course is good for you. I imagine you're still a bit sleepy. Later on if you wish we'll let you have a bite to eat. Perhaps some gelatin would taste good."

Millie nodded, then noticed something familiar on the table by her bed. There stood her little bird looking as if he were grinning, and behind him was the beautiful blue feather in the white vase. Giving in to the drowsy feeling that still lingered, she  closed her eyes. But before falling back to sleep she smiled, thinking of her two gifts from the Sunshine Box. How nice it was to have them nearby!

Chapter 8

IN THE HOSPITAL

As her days in the hospital lengthened, Millie began to miss familiar things from home. She particularly missed the grandfather clock that stood in a corner of the hallway near the front door. It was tall and made of cherry wood that was deeply polished in rich tones of brown. Touching it revealed a satin smoothness matched by no other piece of furniture in the whole house. Millie had never fully understood why the clock was always called a grandfather clock, unless perhaps it had been her grandfather's clock at one time. She knew it was very old and therefore could have been her grandfather's, since he himself had also been very old. In fact, he had been so old that he had finally passed on and now lived happily in heaven.

Millie wondered about the stories the grandfather clock might tell if it were only able to speak. She loved to stare into its glass door and watch the slow movement of the golden pendulum as it swung back and forth with a rhythmic, methodical tick-tock, tick-tock. Upon the arrival of each hour it would burst forth with deep, echoing ding-dongs. Sometimes Millie woke in the middle of the night and she would hear the grandfather clock slice through the quiet household as it struck the hour. Like a faithful friend, the clock's steady performance gave Millie a secure feeling of belonging.

Several days went by. Each morning Millie woke up feeling a little better. Mamma and Papa spent lots of time with Millie—sometimes reading with her, sometimes telling stories from long ago, and sometimes playing games. The nurses were kind and friendly, and Dr. Neils stopped in quite often. He liked to gently tease Millie, but he also kept a cautious eye on her condition. Sometimes

Benjamin came with Mamma or Papa for a visit. Soon Millie began to long for the time when she could go home.

One day, Anna Sue came along with Mamma for a visit. What a special day! Seeing Anna Sue's bright smile and hearing all of the news from school was a rare treat.

"I have something for you, Millie," Anna Sue said with excitement. "Our teacher said maybe you would enjoy drawing now that you are going to be well again. I miss seeing the pretty pictures you used to draw. And Benjamin said that you would especially like to draw with colored pencils. So our class went together to buy these colored pencils for you. Look—they're in this box. See, all the colors are here!"

She handed the box to a very surprised Millie.

"Oh, Anna Sue, how wonderful! Thank you, thank you so very much. I can hardly believe it! I've wanted colored pencils for so long!" Millie exclaimed in delight.

"What will you draw first, Millie?" Anna Sue asked.

Millie carefully examined each pencil as she pondered Anna Sue's question. Then she said, "Oh, I know. I know exactly what I'll draw first of all! I'll draw a picture of my beautiful blue feather from my Sunshine Box. Papa suggested that the first time we saw it."

Millie looked over at the white vase that held her blue feather. But the feather was gone! The vase stood completely empty. Millie was very sad. Anna Sue and Mamma began to search for the feather, looking all around the tabletop, on the floor underneath the table, and even under Millie's bed. But the feather could not be found.

Millie, now greatly distraught, shook her head as she wondered what could have happened to her feather. Then a strange sensation came over her and she began to giggle.

"Whatever is so funny, Millie?" asked Mamma. Just then a nurse walked into the room to announce the end of visiting hours. She looked curiously at Millie, who was still giggling.

"Something is tickling my feet!" Millie said between giggles. The nurse quickly pulled back Millie's covers. And there was the blue feather twisting beneath Millie's wiggling toes.

"Why, of all things!" exclaimed the nurse. "What kind of magic is this?" Anna Sue and Millie continued to laugh and giggle in delight.

Mamma smiled. "Millie, it's so nice to hear you laugh. It's been a long time since we've heard you giggle. Perhaps your feather has a mission of happiness to accomplish."

The nurse lifted the feather from the end of the bed and placed it carefully back in its vase on the bedside table. "I must be working too hard! Or else my mind is playing tricks on me, because it sure looked like that feather was tickling your toes!"

"It's all right," Millie explained to the nurse. "Maybe my feather's not just a blue feather. Maybe I should call it my Fun Feather. It came from my Sunshine Box and it's putting sunshine inside of me—just like my little bird."

"Remember the day you received your Sunshine Box, Millie?" said Mamma. "And I told you the Proverbs verse about how a merry heart does good like a medicine?"

Millie nodded.

"And we certainly like good medicine in this hospital," said the nurse with a wink.

Before Anna Sue left, Millie thanked her again for bringing the wonderful colored pencils. She promised to draw pictures for Anna Sue to take to her classmates.

Time seemed to pass very slowly in the hospital, with each day longer than the one before. But now that Millie had new colored pencils, maybe time would pass quickly. She went to sleep looking forward to the next day and drawing with her new pencils.

Millie ate breakfast quickly the next morning and

waited for the nurse to straighten her bed. Now Millie was ready to begin. She was going to make a picture of her Fun Feather in the white vase. She chose several colored pencils—light blue, dark blue, and even a white pencil to use on the light areas. A deliberately long look at the feather helped Millie fully grasp the outline of its shape. Then, quickly but precisely, Millie began to draw.

The Fun Feather was lovely—so light and delicate. Today it seemed to actually shimmer with silvery highlights. When Millie glanced out the window she understood why the feather appeared unusually clear and bright in color. Outside, the falling snow filled the sky, and the whiteness of snowflakes blowing across the window surface illuminated the whole room with a bright glow.

Millie smiled at the effect this had on her drawing. Then suddenly her eyes opened wide and her hand froze on the paper, for she saw something most startling! The Fun Feather gave an unmistakable flutter and then lightly lifted itself right out of the white vase and floated off through the air from one corner of the room to the next. Millie's eyes followed the feather up and down, over and

around, as she was completely caught up in the wonder of that almost unbelievable moment. Then, just as suddenly as it had taken flight, her Fun Feather quickly returned to its vase and eased itself into its former position, all settled to pose once again. Millie couldn't believe her eyes. Then Little Bitty Bird's yellow bill began to open and he let out a series of squeaky squawks.

"Little Bitty Bird, did you see that? Did you see what I just saw?" Millie asked in great confusion. "Was I dreaming?"

Little Bitty Bird cocked his head slightly to one side as he studied the feather. "No, Millie, you weren't dreaming," he answered in his high-pitched voice. "I saw just what you saw and if I am wide awake, then so are you! Don't let the Fun Feather worry you. That feather is full of bright ideas! It simply wants to share some fun with you. After all, you must remember where you first found your feather." As if on cue the Fun Feather jumped out of the vase and tickled Millie right on the tip of her nose! She laughed loudly and continued giggling as the Fun Feather wiggled its way back to the vase, resuming its beautiful pose.

The nurse entered the room and gave Millie a quizzical look. "Millie, have you had a visitor here this early in the day?" she asked.

"No," said Millie. "Mamma won't be here until the afternoon."

"How strange. I thought I heard voices in here! My imagination must be playing tricks on me again," said the nurse with a frown. Millie smiled politely, holding in her laughter and not daring to look at Little Bitty Bird or the Fun Feather.

"Oh well," said the nurse. "Here's something for you." She handed her a letter. Millie had received many nice get-well cards from the church family, friends from school, her teacher, and some of her relatives from far away. Widow Long had been especially kind, sending a pleasant card of some sort every week. But receiving a letter was something new and exciting!

Millie took the letter and examined it with great curiosity. It was from Robert Wesley. How grand! How wonderful! Robert Wesley had printed it very neatly so that she could read it without help. There was so much news—all about his trip on the train to the army camp, the training he was getting

in order to become a good soldier, his hopes for helping to end the horrible war, and how much he missed everyone at home. Best of all, he reminded Millie how he wanted her to get well soon since he would be coming home for a visit at Christmastime.

Millie felt good inside. The day was turning out to be such fun! She read Robert Wesley's letter once more before she laid it on the bedside table. Then she gave the Fun Feather an approving grin, picked up her pencils, and continued working on her drawing.

Just as she finished the last bit of color on what had turned out to be a truly fine picture, Mamma arrived. "I'm early, Millicent Ruth," Mamma said, "but with this snow coming down so heavily, I thought I should come right away. Besides that, today is another day for you to open one of the gifts from your Sunshine Box!"

Mamma took off her warm coat and sat on the edge of Millie's bed. Together they pulled off the lid of the beautiful Sunshine Box.

"Which gift is it, Mamma?" Millie looked at the four remaining gifts.

"Well now, I believe it's the one in the yellow

tissue paper. Look at its tag and read what it says," Mamma answered.

Millie read the tag tied to the small square box. "To be opened on an especially happy day."

"And Millie dear, today is an especially happy day because Dr. Neils tells us that you may come home tomorrow morning. Isn't that wonderful news?"

"Oh yes, Mamma, that is wonderful news! And Mamma, today has already been a happy day.

Millie was just about to tell Mamma about her funny experience with the feather when all at once she realized that she was still holding the unwrapped gift from her Sunshine Box. Together Mamma and Millie untied the gold bow and took off the tissue.

"It's a tiny cup and saucer!" Millie said as she held it for Mamma to examine.

"Why, it's a real china cup! What lovely pink rosebuds! You'll want to be careful; it could break

Look at what came in the mail! It's a letter from Robert Wesley. Look here too, Mamma. I've drawn my first picture with my new colored pencils!"

As Mamma admired the drawing, Millie told her how she wanted to give this first picture to Anna Sue to share with her classmates.

"That is a lovely thought, dear," agreed Mamma. "They will certainly be happy to receive such a nice drawing."

quite easily. And look here, Millie, see what's written on the cup."

Millie read the elaborate, hand-painted letters: "My cup is full and running over."

"That's one of my favorite verses from the Bible, Millie," Mamma exclaimed. "It's surely meaningful for you and for all of us who love you. We've had our prayers answered. God has taken care of you and you are going to be completely well again. We're so full of happiness that we're like a cup that's running over!"

"I understand what you mean, Mamma!" Millie said. "I have so much happiness inside me that it's more than I can keep—it's running over. That's what would happen if we tried to fill this cup with a whole teapot full of tea—it would run over!"

Millie smiled as Mamma carefully put the cup and saucer back into its box. She lay down again with her head against the pillows. She was happy, but there did exist one unsolved problem. A question troubled her more and more each day.

"Mamma, I just don't understand it," Millie said.

"What don't you understand, Millie dear?" Mamma asked.

"It's my Sunshine Box—who gave it to me? And how will I ever say 'thank you' when I don't know who gave me such a wonderful box with all of these nice gifts?"

"It is a mystery," Mamma agreed. "Perhaps we'll discover the answer to those questions when all of the gifts have been opened. Until that time, I suppose you'll just have to be patient. But you can be thankful within your heart."

Later, after Mamma had gone home, Millie lay in bed watching the snow falling outside the window. Somewhere, someplace, someone out there was giving Millie a lot of happiness. Someday she hoped she would be able to say thank you to the giver of her mysterious, marvelous Sunshine Box. Tomorrow would soon come, however, and just knowing she would go home brought a perfect ending to a delightfully happy day.

Chapter 9

A TREASURED VISIT

ome at last, Millie lay in her bed comfortably warm under her pile of patchwork quilts. She enjoyed looking out her window with its frosty edges. Gray puffs of smoke spiraled through the clear winter sky from the snow-covered chimney on top of Widow Long's house. Still firm and solid in their shape, icicles hung in an uneven row along the base of the roof. Hearing Benjamin call out "Good-bye!" as he left for school, slamming the front door, made Millie wish that she could run after him. How she wanted to call out, "Wait for me, I'm coming too!"

Millie was thankful to be back in her own room, but now that she felt better it was hard to spend long hours in bed. The hospital visit was over, the operation had been a success, and Millie was ready to be well!

Thanksgiving had come and gone. Millie's family enjoyed a delicious feast despite the food shortages caused by the war. With Millie on the mend, they had good reason to celebrate and give thanks. Now as Christmas drew near, the house buzzed with excitement. But Millie felt a strange emptiness gnawing deep inside. She knew she shouldn't feel sorry for herself. She thought about her Sunshine Box and its gifts, cards and visits from her friends, letters from Robert Wesley, news from school shared by Anna Sue, Mamma and Papa's loving care, and hours spent in quiet play with Benjamin—with all of this, she really shouldn't feel sorry for herself. She knew she should be thankful. But all these weeks in bed were hard, and Millie's spirits were drooping.

Suddenly Benjamin burst back through the front door and ran up the stairs to Millie's room. "I have an important message!" he sputtered,

nearly out of breath. "Widow Long has invited you to spend the morning with her over at her house! And Mamma and Papa say it's okay! Papa's going to bundle you up and carry you over there. Widow Long has an armchair all fixed up with pillows and blankets for you. Isn't that something? You're sure lucky! Wish I could go!"

Millie's gloom disappeared! She didn't even know how to express how grand she suddenly felt, but going to Widow Long's for a visit would be a delight!

"Well, don't just lie there with your mouth open—say something!" barked her brother. "Anyway, I have to hurry now or I'll miss the school bus!" Benjamin clambered back down the stairs, his boot buckles jiggling and jangling as he jumped two steps at a time. Millie slowly raised herself up in her bed as a broad smile spread across her face.

After Millie finished breakfast, Papa and Mamma bundled her up warmly with her jacket and hood buttoned securely over her nightgown and bathrobe. Around all those layers Mamma wrapped the woolly blue-and-red afghan from the sofa in the living room. Then Papa hoisted Millie onto his back and carried her to Widow Long's home.

Millie had thought that being bundled and carried was great foolishness. Surely she could just put on her snow pants and boots and walk over to Widow Long's as she had always done in the past! But, much to her surprise, just taking a few steps across the rug to her chair by the door left Millie feeling overwhelmingly dizzy. Her knees seemed to be made of rubber! Mamma and Papa chuckled as they explained that it was quite normal to feel weak after having spent so many weeks in bed. After that, Millie decided that being carried to Widow Long's might not be so bad after all.

"Your strength will return," Mamma assured, "but it will take time and patience."

"Time and patience," thought Millie, frowning. "That's all I seem to hear anymore." But her dismal thoughts vanished as Papa carried her out the door.

It was warm and cozy inside Widow Long's house. A welcoming fire crackled in the fireplace and the delicious smell of cinnamon wafted from the direction of the kitchen. Even though it was daytime, a little candle flickered cheerfully beside Widow Long's old leather Bible on the coffee table.

Millie loved Widow Long's "parlor," as the widow called it. It was full of pictures, books, knickknacks, and furniture of the past. And everything had a story behind it. Millie knew that if she asked the right questions, the widow would spin one of her tales from the olden days that Millie so loved to hear.

Papa said good-bye and left Millie comfortably settled in the armchair, resting against an assortment of old-fashioned pillows. The pillows felt luscious and slippery, covered with satin pillowcases and smelling of old English lavender. Millie and Widow Long chatted for quite a while as the widow rocked in her chair by the fireplace, a gray knitted shawl draped around her shoulders. It had been such a long time since they had enjoyed a good visit! Widow Long began relating a funny story about her grandfather, who got caught in a deep snowdrift as he gathered maple sugar from the trees in the woods a little north of town. Then the old widow interrupted her story to shuffle into the kitchen and fetch whatever it was that smelled so wonderful. The heavy iron door of the old wood stove creaked as it opened.

Widow Long returned shortly, carrying a plate of steaming hot cinnamon buns. On top of each bun sat a sprinkling of brown sugar and a circle of melting butter. The story of Widow Long's grandfather was somehow forgotten as Millie and the widow enjoyed their delicious treat.

"Oh, dear me, Millie, I am so forgetful," muttered Widow Long. "I left the teapot in the kitchen. Excuse me one moment and I'll go get it. These buns are never quite as tasty as they should be without a good hot cup of tea!"

Off she shuffled again, only in greater haste this time. Millie smothered a giggle because the old widow truly was forgetful. When Widow Long returned, Millie was surprised to notice the teacups and saucers on the tray beside the teapot. How familiar they looked! Then Millie remembered...

"Guess what, Widow Long! I have a new cup and saucer all my very own. They're just exactly like your cups and saucers!" Millie exclaimed.

"Well now, that's a curious thing, isn't it! Tell me, Millie, how did you get your cup and saucer?" asked Widow Long.

Millie told Widow Long the story of her Sunshine Box. Widow Long listened with interest. Millie hesitated for a moment, wondering if she should share the adventures she had enjoyed with Little Bitty Bird and the Fun Feather. Behind Widow Long's funny gold-rimmed glasses Millie glimpsed a twinkle in her eyes. Without hesitating any longer, Millie went ahead with her story. The widow frowned a time or two, then smiled a time or two, but listened most intently to all that Millie said.

"Well now, Millie, that's a most fascinating story!" said the widow.

"But you do believe it, don't you? Everything I've told you about the Little Bitty Bird and my Fun Feather has really happened!" Millie said with determination.

"Millie, my child, I understand completely," said Widow Long as she patted the calico cat that had curled itself up in her lap for a comfortable morning nap. "Did you know, Millie, that our heavenly Father has promised to give to us all we ever need? Let me tell you a story. Once when I was a very little girl, I needed to be loved very much. You see, my mother and father were very, very wealthy people, and they were very, very important people. I was their only child, but somehow they never found much time for me. Oh, they gave me everything a little girl would ever want—toys to play with, pretty clothes to wear, everything and anything I ever wanted." The widow paused here and then added, "Everything except love. But then Mr. Smitty taught me something."

"Who was Mr. Smitty, Widow Long?" Millie asked.

"Who was Mr. Smitty? Why Millie, Mr. Smitty was everything wonderful that could ever happen to a lonely little girl. He was the man who took care of the gardens around our big house. That in itself wasn't so important to me. It was what happened between Mr. Smitty and me that became important. I used to tag along, following behind him wherever he worked. And all that time he would either be whistling a tune or telling me a tale that just had to be unbelievable. But he could always make it believable! He took me into the wonderful land of pretending. Our roses became beautiful maidens; our hollyhocks became the homes of the elves; our pansies became the colored pools in which the fairies could swim; and Mr. Smitty taught me about love."

Old Widow Long paused for a moment to gaze into the fireplace. "Do you understand, Millie? Mr. Smitty taught me about love by sharing a wonderful gift that God had given to him—the gift of love itself. And Mr. Smitty showed me this love by taking time to teach me how to pretend. I suppose pretending could be harmful, but when the time is right, pretending can bring great happiness. Oh, yes, Millie child, I do believe your stories about your Sunshine Box!"

After eating another bun, Millie licked off her sticky fingers. The tea was cooling off so she drank what was left in her cup. Widow Long's stories were always fun to hear, but this one was different. It gave Millie lots to think about. In fact, for the first

time she was beginning to understand the mystery of her Sunshine Box.

Millie put the teacup back down on its saucer. It wasn't exactly the same as her cup and saucer after all, for this cup did not have a Bible verse written on it. Once again, Millie felt full and running over with happiness. And she could see that Widow Long was also happy. The kind old woman was quiet now, lost in her memories, smiling contentedly as she rocked back and forth in her wicker rocking chair.

Before long, Papa returned to take Millie home. After he deposited her back on her bed and Mamma took off all her wraps, Benjamin brought her the Sunshine Box.

"Millie, do you remember that one of the gift tags said, 'For your first good day out of bed away from home'?" Benjamin asked.

"Yes!" Millie exclaimed. "Going to the hospital didn't really count, but today has been a good day and I was out of bed away from home!"

"Wonder what it'll be?" Benjamin asked. "Look—it's the round one in the purple tissue paper."

"Whatever it is, it'll be wonderful!" Millie declared. "Here, Benjamin, you open this one." Benjamin accepted Millie's offer enthusiastically, for he always enjoyed surprises. It was a mirror— a most elaborate mirror with a golden frame of delicately carved rosebuds similar to the rosebuds that circled her teacup. The back of the mirror held a wire stand that could be pulled out to hold the mirror upright on a table. Millie loved it! Benjamin thought it was nice too, but decided it was strictly a gift for a girl.

Soon it was bedtime. Outside, the stars sparkled and the moonlight shone brightly through Millie's window. Her new mirror caught the reflection of the shadows and light in the bedroom. She looked into the mirror, and for one quick instant saw the form of a little girl running between rosebushes and tall hollyhocks. Was she pretending, or was this the beginning of a dream? Millie thought about her treasured time with the old widow, but then her eyes closed and she soon fell fast asleep.

Chapter 10

CHRISTMAS DELIGHT

"Christmas cheer, Christmas cheer, Christmas cheer!" Papa sang this funny little song each morning to wake the children. Christmas was coming and the joy and merriment of the holiday season rang throughout the house. Now that most of Millie's pain from her illness was gone, she felt eager to participate in the festivities. But try as she might, the weakness remained. She still had to spend many hours in bed, but looked forward to the special time each day when Papa would carry her down to the living-room sofa.

Dr. Neils continued to stop by once or twice each week to examine and encourage Millie. "Your strength will return, Millie girl, but it's very important to wait patiently," the kindly doctor said. "The time will come when you won't tire so easily. When you've grown stronger you'll be able to run and jump and play like all your friends at school."

Then Dr. Neils winked and sneaked a stick of gum into Millie's mouth when Mamma wasn't looking. Mamma had always been strict about store-bought sweets.

Millie thought how grand it would be if she could be well and strong by Christmas Eve. So much would happen on that special day! In the morning Papa and Benjamin would leave for the wooded hillside behind the Powell farm to chop down a carefully chosen Christmas tree. The afternoon would be busy with baking Christmas cookies and decorating the tree with colorful balls and trinkets from the attic.

The best part of Christmas Eve came in the evening when they all gathered in the little white-steepled church for a worship service with candles glowing, happy voices singing carols, and the wondrous Bible story of the very first Christmas.

Millie got goose bumps when she thought about it. She must try to rest a lot, eat well, and take her medicine. It would be horrible to miss what had to be the most wonderful time of year.

Benjamin's constant reminders of Robert Wesley's promised Christmas visit didn't help matters. When Papa sang about Christmas cheer, Benjamin would add, "Christmas cheer, Christmas cheer, Robert Wesley is almost here, almost here."

Widow Long was busy next door. Millie looked down from her bedroom window and into the widow's living-room window to spy a marble-topped table stacked high with brightly wrapped gifts. Mamma said the old widow hand-made most of her gifts and that she gave more to poor and needy families than anyone could ever imagine.

Catching glimpses of Widow Long's gifts and smelling Mamma's plum pudding gave Millie an idea. Actually, it was not completely her own idea. Little Bitty Bird had shared the secret with her, and from then on Millie became quite involved in the excitement of the Christmas season. It was the new mirror from the Sunshine Box that Little Bitty Bird had told her about. With it Millie could see many wonderful scenes. At first she only saw her own face—her big blue eyes that stood out against her very pale complexion, and her blonde hair that had grown quite long the last few months.

"But Millie, look harder! You're missing so much," screeched Little Bitty Bird.

Millie looked and looked. Still she saw only her face and nothing more. The Fun Feather floated over to rest on top of Millie's head. It wiggled in its own frivolous manner, laughing at Millie for missing what even it could apparently see.

Then suddenly it happened! When Millie pulled the mirror up as close to her face as possible and glared into it with determination, all at once she caught an eyeful of an outrageously marvelous sight! She saw a huge orange sun over a wooded hillside where Papa and Benjamin were chopping down a stately fir tree. What a remarkable scene and what a remarkable mirror!

"Now draw it, silly girl, draw it!" commanded the bird in a shrill squawk.

Millie, at last understanding Little Bitty Bird's idea, set out her colored pencils and began to draw an absolutely delightful picture. When she finished, she became almost frantic to begin a second drawing. Day after day, the wonderful mirror came forth with beautiful scenes for Millie to create. It was not long before she had a pile of pictures: one of Benjamin flying a kite that chased billowy clouds high above the ground; one of Mamma hanging up the washing on the clothesline that hung between the two apple trees; one of Widow Long pruning her rosebushes with a calico cat sitting beside her; one of Papa in his black preacher's robe preaching a sermon about God's love; and one of Robert Wesley sitting on the side of the pasture fence playing his dulcimer. Millie could almost hear those sweet notes! The pile of drawings grew. What a wonderful mirror to have discovered in the Sunshine Box!

"Little Bitty Bird, now I have an idea!" Millie said. "Everyone has been so kind to me for such a long time. I want to give all these drawings to my family and friends for Christmas. They won't be just Christmas gifts— they'll be thank-you gifts, too!"

"Sounds like you could call them love gifts," said Little Bitty Bird thoughtfully.

"Yes, I suppose so," Millie replied.

Fun Feather gave a quick jump into the air to show that it also agreed.

Millie looked over each drawing carefully. She thought about the mirror, then smiled in Little Bitty Bird's direction. She felt warm inside as she remembered Widow Long's story about Mr. Smitty and their shared world of pretending. Pretending could be useful...and some pretending should be kept secret. Millie and Little Bitty Bird and the Fun Feather would keep this secret—their Christmas secret!

On the day before Christmas Eve, Dr. Neils made a bargain

with Millie. After examining her quite thoroughly, he bent his head down to Millie and whispered, "I'll tell you what, Millie—if you will promise to save me a bowl of your mamma's plum pudding, I'll give you my permission to spend Christmas Eve in church!"

Wide-eyed and happy, Millie whispered back, "I sure will! I promise I will!"

Christmas Eve came and Papa carried Millie to the sofa, where she shared fully in the delights of the day. The plum pudding and cookies smelled so festive! Soon red-cheeked Papa and Benjamin carried the fir tree into the living room. As the afternoon grew dim, the tree glowed with tinseled glory, draped in glittering lights and ornaments of vibrant colors. Still, the best part of the day was yet to come. Millie tried hard to be patient during supper. At last patience gave way to joy when she heard the sound of sleigh bells from outside. Benjamin ran to the front window.

"It's Robert Wesley!" he announced excitedly. "It's Robert Wesley with his pa's horse and sleigh!" Benjamin rushed to the door, opened it wide, and jumped down the snow-covered porch steps right into Robert Wesley's big bear hug of a welcome.

Millie wanted to see him too! Then Papa lifted her up and carried her to the open door. Millie reached out her arms, and as Robert Wesley entered the house, he took her from Papa and held her in a big, warm hug. Mamma closed the door and looked at Robert Wesley with tears shining in her eyes. Millie realized she too had tears streaming down her face, but they were happy tears. It was a joyous reunion!

Suddenly everyone started talking at once. Papa said, "Welcome home, soldier!" and clapped Robert Wesley heartily on the back.

"You look wonderful in your uniform!" Mamma exclaimed.

"Do you like being in the army?" Benjamin wondered.

"I'm so glad you're here," added Millie, nestling her head against his shoulder.

"I'm glad to be here, too," Robert Wesley answered. "How's my Millie girl?"

"I'm feeling lots better," she answered.

"Yes—I can see that," he agreed.

"Dr. Neils even said I can go to church tonight!" she added.

"Great! That's the best news I could hear!" said Robert Wesley with a big smile.

On and on they chattered until suddenly the grandfather clock struck the hour.

"Dear me," Mamma exclaimed. "We've almost forgotten the time! We must hurry or we'll be late for church! Papa, Benjamin, hurry and get our wraps." As they all bundled up it was quickly agreed that Mamma and Papa would drive on ahead while Millie and Benjamin rode in the sleigh with Robert Wesley. What fun! Dressed warmly in her snowsuit and wrapped in a plaid blanket, Millie sat on one side of Robert Wesley and Benjamin sat on the other. Off they went with the horse trotting briskly through the crisp night air. Millie felt that this just had to be the best Christmas Eve ever.

The candles glowed inside the little church, casting a warm yellow light around a room full of fir branches and holly. Young and old gathered as one big family to celebrate the birth of the Christ child. Voices lifted in songs of joy and praise. Prayers of thanksgiving were given to the heavenly Father for His Son, Jesus,

the perfect love gift to the whole world.

All of a sudden Millie remembered what Little Bitty Bird had said about the drawings she had made for Christmas gifts. He had called them love gifts. She understood that God's gift of Jesus was a perfect love gift, but it made her feel good to think of her gifts as love gifts too. She felt happy inside knowing that she was following God's loving example.

Papa read the beautiful Christmas story from the Bible. Then the elders of the church put out

the candles along each pew, leaving only the candle in the front of the church still burning. Millie watched in awe as Papa explained that the single candle represented Jesus as the one and only light of the world—a light of hope for every person.

In the hushed silence, Robert Wesley walked to the front of the congregation. Standing in the light of that one candle, he played "Silent Night, Holy Night" on his dulcimer. Millie thought she would never again hear such beautiful music.

As the last note rang from the strings, Papa began to pray.

"Thank You, Lord, for sending us the wonderful gift of Your Son, Jesus. Thank You that our country is still free and that we can worship You without fear. Please, Lord, bring a speedy end to the terrible war that has cost so many lives. Please bring peace on earth. Lord, we ask You to protect Robert Wesley, who's leaving for Europe to join his four brothers on the battlefield. Watch over and protect them all, we pray. We thank and praise You, Father, for the beauty and wonder of this holy night, in Jesus' name. Amen."

Millie had been feeling drowsy, but all at once she opened her eyes and stared at Robert Wesley. Papa must have been mistaken, or had she misunderstood his prayer? Robert Wesley couldn't go to war—not yet—not where all the fighting was hurting and killing people—not now!

Papa finished praying, then Robert Wesley spoke. "None of us is happy about the war. But we can always be happy in the love God has shown to us by giving us His Son, Jesus. I have faith in God, and I believe He will go with me as I leave all of you. So let's have a merry Christmas—a Christmas full of cheer. Please join me in one more song."

They all sang "Faith Is the Victory." Millie didn't completely understand the words, but she could feel the strength that came as they were sung. Robert Wesley's face glowed with peace and joy as he played those last notes on his dulcimer. Farmer Powell and his wife looked sad but brave, and very proud of their youngest son. Then, in the light of that one candle, Papa and Robert Wesley embraced right in front of all of the people of the church. Millie knew she would never ever forget that Christmas Eve—not ever.

Chapter 11

THE TUNNEL AND THE TREE

Christmas Day came and went in an excited blur of merriment and joy. Millie placed the figure of the Christ child in the manger of the tiny nativity scene that always held the place of honor under the tree. Then the family sang "O Little Town of Bethlehem" before opening their gifts. Millie's favorite gift was a jigsaw puzzle with hundreds of tiny pieces. Mamma said Millie could put it together on a large tray right on her bed! But Millie knew her favorite Christmas memory would be of the joy in the faces of her loved ones as they looked at the colored pencil drawings that she had crafted so carefully, then rolled and tied with festive ribbon. That she had drawn the pictures from scenes in her wonderful mirror remained a secret among Millie, Little Bitty Bird, and the Fun Feather.

On New Year's Day Millie woke early. The house was quiet, for the rest of the family was still asleep. Millie nestled under the covers in her cold bedroom. It wouldn't warm up until Papa shoveled coal into the furnace. Millie's nose was as cold as a small snowball. The outer edges of her pillowcase felt like the smooth surface of a frozen lake.

All at once Millie became aware of a most marvelous smell. Sniffing, she decided the smell was both delectable and familiar. That was when she wondered if her cup and saucer from the Sunshine Box were no ordinary cup and saucer— for in the cup was hot cocoa! Forgetting her cold room, Millie sat up to look at the fingers of steam that rose from the cup. What a strange mystery! Mamma had made cocoa for Millie and Benjamin the night before. And Millie had asked for a second cup, since there was nothing quite like hot cocoa. But Mamma had said she would have to remember

to buy more cocoa the next time she went to the grocery store since that was the last of what she had.

"So," Millie said out loud, "where has this cocoa come from?" Furthermore, who had poured it into her cup? Certainly she would have heard if someone had entered her room. Millie quickly dismissed all of these questions. After all, the cocoa was obviously meant for her since it was in her cup. And it would be much better if she enjoyed it while it was still hot. So drink it she did—it was the most delicious cocoa she had ever tasted!

As soon as the cocoa was gone, Millie wished for more. As she peered down into her cup, her mouth dropped open in disbelief. How could it be? Her cup was refilling itself with cocoa! Impossible, but there it was, full again to the very top and looking so wonderfully tasty that Millie had no choice but to drink it up.

Until then, Millie hadn't noticed anything terribly unusual about the cup and saucer from her Sunshine Box. She knew that she needed to handle this treasure with care—it was so fragile and lovely. She had long since memorized the Bible verse lettered between the rosebuds on the cup.

With the psalmist from the Bible, Millie too could say, "My cup is running over." With all the happiness that the Sunshine Box brought to her, she felt like a cup filled with joy—so much joy that it was running over.

Millie sipped the marvelous cocoa, then shook her head. She felt bewildered and happy and amazed all at the same time. Since she'd been ill so many unbelievable things had happened! She looked over at her beautiful Sunshine Box sitting in the morning light. It was as if Millie's pain had slowly melted away with the opening of each gift. Little Bitty Bird was now her good friend; the Fun Feather tickled its merry way into her heart; the mirror had shown her many enjoyable scenes; and her cup and saucer reminded her of overflowing joy—all of these gifts had pulled Millie into the most amazing adventures imaginable! Her heart filled with excitement and anticipation as she remembered that inside the Sunshine Box, two gifts still remained to be opened. Who could have given her the Sunshine Box? She had some suspicions, but as yet there was no way to know for sure. Whenever Millie mentioned this, Mamma would say, "Millie, you need to learn patience. Someday I'm sure you'll know who to thank for your Sunshine Box." Patient or not, Millie still wondered.

Her thoughts were interrupted by Benjamin. "Millie, it isn't fair!" he complained.

"What's not fair?" she asked, with her blankets pulled close to her chin.

"You've had cocoa and I haven't, and Mamma said we didn't have any cocoa left last night." Benjamin looked silly in his baggy pajamas and hair sticking out, but his face was scowling darkly. Millie wondered if he would even believe her if she told him about her special cup. Chocolate was Benjamin's favorite. How could she possibly explain?

Just then Mamma entered the bedroom and greeted both children with a cheerful "Good morning!" Benjamin started to complain, but before he had a chance, Mamma began to speak. "Millie, today we have a surprise for you. Dr. Neils said it would be good for you to start doing your schoolwork since you're feeling so much better. I spoke with your teacher, and Anna Sue will bring your school books home. Isn't that exciting?"

"Oh Mamma, that is exciting!" exclaimed Millie. "I'm so happy! Maybe it won't be long until I get to go back to school." Millie wished her legs were strong enough to climb out of bed and jump up and down. She looked at Benjamin, who was standing with arms folded across his chest and still looking rather unhappy about the cocoa.

"My, but it does smell good in here!" said Mamma, as if she knew what was troubling Benjamin. "In fact, that reminds me—I got to thinking last night that I just might have another tin of cocoa in the pantry. Benjamin, would you like to go look before you get dressed?" Benjamin appeared most willing. Mamma smiled as Benjamin bolted from the bedroom with a grin across his face. As Mamma left she turned and winked at Millie. Now

Millie was more puzzled than ever. Did Mamma know something about the mysterious cups of cocoa?

Little Bitty Bird began to wink, too. Actually, Millie decided he was blinking at the bright sunshine. And high time, too, for he had snoozed through the morning's events. Now he began to wiggle and shake himself. "Good morning, Millie girl," he chirped. "Look at me, I'm wide awake and ready for a great day!"

"Oh yes, Little Bitty Bird, I see you're awake and it is a great day! Anna Sue is bringing my school books to me after school today. Isn't that great?"

Little Bitty Bird stretched his fluffy neck. "Well, I suppose it depends upon how you look at it. Books seem to be important to people, but I don't care much for books. Now if you were talking about a branch on the maple tree, that would be different!"

Millie laughed in an understanding way and said, "Just the same, Little Bitty Bird, I can hardly wait! I'm going to work very hard with my school books so when I go back to school again I won't be too far behind the other children."

The little bird looked down. "I suppose you want to go back to school, Millie."

"Yes, I do! Ever since Christmas that's all I've been able to think about. But my legs are still wobbly when I try to walk. Dr. Neils says that's because I've been in bed for so long. I can't wait until I can walk again. I can't go back to school until then."

"Perhaps I could help," suggested Little Bitty Bird.

"Oh, Little Bitty Bird, you're so kind, but how could you possibly help?"

He lifted his feathered head and answered, "I know of a way. It might take time, but it could be done. But we'd need to keep it secret—so you could surprise everybody."

"Really? Little Bitty Bird, could you really help me? How?" Millie asked.

"Simple! Simply simple! The way I see it, you just need to get your strength back. Therefore, you must come with me to the Lemon Tree."

"To what lemon tree? Little Bitty Bird, that's silly. There aren't any lemon trees here. Besides, it's wintertime—even if there were a lemon tree, how could there be lemons?"

"Never fear, Millie dear. Just do as I say and you'll see. First open that window. Then you need to think very hard to become my size. Then you can hop on my back."

"But what about my breakfast? Mamma will bring it soon," Millie protested.

"No need to worry, Millie. We'll be back in time. First things first, I always say."

Since Millie remembered her previous adventure with Little Bitty Bird, it wasn't difficult for her to think hard enough to shrink from her normal size down to Little Bitty Bird size. Then she climbed onto his downy-soft back and held on tight as Little Bitty Bird raised his wings and soared through the open bedroom window.

It was a splendid day! The sun shining across the snow-covered hills caused the world below to look like a magnificent pie topped with foamy meringue. They enjoyed the freedom of the wind as they swooped up and down through the air. Little Bitty Bird peeped a tune of melodious chirps and Millie savored the feeling of wind blowing

through her hair. It was not long before Little Bitty Bird said, "Hold on, Millie! We're going to dive down to a landing spot."

Millie obeyed, clutching Little Bitty Bird's neck. With a thump and a thud they landed on a small rock that was partially covered with snow. Millie gazed at the strange surroundings. Behind them stood a dense forest, and in front lay a long valley that stretched endlessly between rolling white hills. But she didn't see any lemon trees.

"Now stay on my back, Millie. There's a bit of walking to be done before we reach the tunnel," squawked Little Bitty Bird. Millie wondered why they were going to a tunnel. But then the whole idea of looking for a lemon tree in the middle of winter was outrageous anyway. One more ridiculous idea made little difference. As they entered the forest, Millie sat silently on Little Bitty Bird's back and tried to wait patiently.

"There, Millie, there it is! Look! See—the opening to the tunnel is hidden between those two fir trees and that clump of white birches. Oh, this is exciting!" Little Bitty Bird cried. Millie felt goose bumps creeping over her arms and legs. "The branches are quite low, so duck your head as we go into the tunnel," peeped Little Bitty Bird. Millie held her head close to his soft back and wondered what would happen next.

"Exciting, exciting! It is exciting!" peeped Little Bitty Bird, his voice echoing.

Darkness shrouded the tunnel, but Millie's eyes gradually grew accustomed to a strange light. Glistening jewels and gems studded the walls and shallow crevasses of the tunnel. Colors of an almost transparent quality sparkled and vibrated off of the clustered stones, giving a luminous, rainbow-like glow to their pathway. Little Bitty Bird burst forth into a lovely song to express his joy and excitement. Rising in a chirping crescendo, his music entwined with the beauty of the tunnel, leaving Millie speechless.

Suddenly the end of the tunnel came into view. Light from outside shone through the arched opening like a giant beam of gold. And there in the snow just outside the tunnel stood the Lemon Tree! It was tall and straight, and its branches bent low under the weight of dozens of beautiful yellow lemons.

Millie tingled with wonder. "You were right, Little Bitty Bird, you were right! There is a Lemon Tree! It's real! You were right!"

"Of course I was right!" he replied. "But we shouldn't waste time, for we must not be gone from home much longer." With a quick hop, Little Bitty Bird flew to the branches of the wonderful Lemon Tree. Millie still clung to his neck.

"Pull off a lemon and eat it up," Little Bitty Bird ordered. "Quickly now—don't waste time!"

"But lemons are sour. I couldn't possibly eat a whole one!" said Millie.

"You want to return to school, don't you?" asked Little Bitty Bird in a squeaky squawk that almost sounded like a scolding.

"Yes," Millie answered meekly.

"Then you must walk again—and in order to do that you must regain your strength. You must at least try, silly girl. Eat! Eat one of the lemons!"

Millie plucked a lemon and sighed. She evidently had no choice. The lemon skin peeled off easily, and with that accomplished Millie touched the lemon with her tongue. To her surprise the lemon was not sour at all, but sweet like candy. Millie quickly devoured the whole lemon. It was scrumptious beyond description!

"Yummy!" Millie said, smacking her lips together. Unable to resist, Millie reached for another lemon. But suddenly she became so tired that it was impossible to hold her eyes open. She never knew for sure what happened next. All she remembered was a blur of color and whirling musical wind. One thing, however, was quite clear. Like the cup of cocoa, that sweet lemon filled Millie with incredible joy.

Chapter 12

SECRETS & FEARS

Millie knew how to keep a secret. After all, with Little Bitty Bird's encouragement she secretly drew the wonderful scenes she discovered inside her magical mirror. And no one learned of her secret until they opened their presents on Christmas Day. Now Millie possessed a new secret. She was gradually gaining back her strength and beginning to walk a little. And it was all because of Little Bitty Bird and the Lemon Tree! They made numerous flights over the hills, down the length of the narrow valley, and through the gem-studded tunnel to the wonderful Lemon Tree. During each visit Millie eagerly gobbled two or three lemons, and each time new strength seemed to pour through her weakened body. She and Little Bitty Bird had to smother their giggles when family or friends asked how she was doing. They both knew it wouldn't be long before she would greatly surprise everyone not only by walking again, but by running and jumping. But until she was strong enough, she and Little Bitty Bird would keep their grand secret.

In the meantime, Millie kept herself busy with schoolwork. She was determined to catch up on everything she had missed during her illness. Mamma helped her, and together they worked industriously. Millie's desire to return to school increased steadily. Each completed lesson brought new excitement. But Mamma would patiently remind her that she couldn't return to school until she was walking again. Then Little Bitty Bird would wink at Millie, and she would grin.

Then one day, something terrible happened. One single phone call plunged the entire household into deep, dark gloom. Papa hadn't meant for Millie to overhear his conversation, but he'd

forgotten to close the door to his study, and Millie's bedroom door was open so she could hear every word that Papa said.

"Why, that's terrible news! You're sure that it's our Robert Wesley? Absolutely positive there isn't a mistake?" Papa's voice sounded tight and strained. After a pause he said with great sadness, "Then I must go and tell the family." Millie heard the phone back drop back to the hook, followed by Papa's slow, heavy steps in the hallway.

Millie cried out, "Papa, what's happened?"

He stopped in front of her doorway and slowly shook his head.

"Papa, what's happened?" Millie repeated.

"Millie, we've just received very bad news," Papa began cautiously. "Our Robert Wesley has been reported missing in action." He paused. "Will this war never end?"

"Missing in action?" cried Millie, tears filling her eyes. "Papa, what does that mean? Is our Robert Wesley—is he dead?"

"He might be dead, Millie. Missing in action means he's lost somewhere and no one knows whether he is alive or not. All we can do is pray."

Tears also filled Papa's eyes. He walked over to Millie, knelt down, and took her in his arms. "He's not dead!" she cried stubbornly. "He can't be— I won't believe it!"

Finally Papa rose and gave her a gentle pat on the head. Poor Papa. She knew he would have to break the dreadful news to Farmer Powell and his wife.

Even Benjamin cried when he heard the news after school. He flopped himself across the foot of Millie's bed, his eyes still misty.

"I won't believe it," Millie asserted once more.

"I won't either," agreed Benjamin. "I just wish there was something we could do!"

Just then Little Bitty Bird ruffled his wings ever so slightly, catching Millie's attention. "Maybe there is," she mused. "Maybe Little Bitty Bird could help us."

"Millie, you're silly! How can a toy bird help?"

"Benjamin, Little Bitty Bird isn't a toy bird! He's real and he can do all sorts of wonderful things. I bet he could find Robert Wesley. You just have to believe me!"

Benjamin sauntered over to Little Bitty Bird.

He picked up the bird and looked it over from head to toe, then shook his head. "Millie, you're really silly!"

"Oh, Benjamin, please believe me," pleaded Millie. "Little Bitty Bird has flown all over my room, and besides that, he even talks!"

"Flying is hard enough to believe, but talking? You must've been dreaming, Millie!" His weak smile failed to hide his hopelessness. "I wish Little Bitty Bird really could fly. And I wish he could find Robert Wesley."

Millie glared at her brother. "You just wait and see, Benjamin. Whether you believe me or not, Little Bitty Bird will find Robert Wesley. I know he will!"

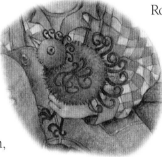

Benjamin set Little Bitty Bird down, then just shook his head and left.

Little Bitty Bird looked at Millie and nodded his tawny brown head in a knowing way. And somehow Millie knew exactly what she needed to do. She reached over from her bed and pulled open the window. "Find Robert Wesley, Little Bitty Bird," she cried. "Then come back to me and tell me he's all right. Hurry, oh please hurry!" Little Bitty Bird launched himself into the gray sky, and a gust of wind lifted him high over the trees. Part of Millie was very sad to see her little friend go, but another part of her was glad—now if only he could find Robert Wesley!

That night after Mamma and Papa and Benjamin and Millie prayed together for Robert Wesley's safety, Millie thought back to the time when her little bird flew bravely through a frightening storm and God's guidance brought them safely home. Now Millie believed with all her heart that God's faithful guidance would take Little Bitty Bird to Robert Wesley. In her heart Millie whispered, "Hurry, Little Bitty Bird! Hurry!"

Chapter 13
MORE MYSTERIES

Millie sat up in bed and looked out her window. For a nice change, the sun was shining and it almost seemed as if spring were in the air. But she knew it was still too early. She would still have to wait for spring to come. Wait. She didn't like that word at all. And yet that's what everyone kept telling her to do. Wait and be patient. Somehow waiting always required more patience than she could muster. It didn't matter whether the waiting was for something happy or a dreaded event; waiting was always an unpleasant task.

Ice cream was always one of the most difficult things to wait for. On a hot summer evening Papa would pour the creamy mixture into the can and fit the can into the wooden bucket. After he packed in rock salt and ice and secured the lid, he would say, "Now you children must help me turn the crank. Wait patiently and we'll soon feast on

vanilla ice cream!" Millie would always sigh. Waiting just took so long.

Now she had to wait for something much more important than ice cream. Day after day Millie waited for the return of Little Bitty Bird. She missed her little friend. But she knew he would come back, and he would bring news of Robert Wesley. If only she didn't have to wait so long. It was harder than anything she'd ever waited for in her whole life! Mamma often said, "No news is good news." Millie wasn't sure about that.

Millie could tell that Benjamin was worried too. He spent more time in her room than ever before. Sometimes they would talk or play games, and sometimes he would stretch himself out at the foot of her bed and just read. Millie tried to remain hopeful, but Benjamin seemed to be giving up. When he asked about Little Bitty Bird's absence,

she reminded him that the bird had flown off to find Robert Wesley. Benjamin simply shrugged his shoulders and went back to reading his book. Millie said no more. He would probably never believe her anyway.

With all this worry, it was a struggle to concentrate on her schoolwork. And without Little Bitty Bird, Millie soon lost all interest in regaining her strength to walk. If only she could go through that magical tunnel, back to the Lemon Tree. Maybe those lemons would give her the energy she needed. But without Little Bitty Bird it was not possible. It was not a happy time for Millie.

One day, Millie felt particularly dismal. March winds had been blowing furiously since early morning, but the day had passed slowly. When Benjamin got home from school, he began to rummage noisily through his closet.

"What are you doing, Benjamin?" called Millie.

"Oh, I have to hurry. The wind's really blowing, so I want to get my kite outside right away. Watch me from your window. Maybe I'll fly it up above the rooftop!"

Millie watched as Benjamin's kite swooped higher and higher. He held the string tightly as he braced himself against the wind. Just as his kite reached the level of her window, a reflection in the window's glass caught Millie's eye. She turned around to see her little round mirror. As usual it sat on her dresser facing the window. But something was different! She walked over and studied it carefully. Sure enough—something was happening inside that mirror! She peered closely at it. Inside she saw what looked like a large wooded area—a forest! Something small seemed to dart in and out of the trees. It was a bird! As it flew nearer, Millie clapped her hand over her mouth to keep from shouting. It was Little Bitty Bird flying fast and furiously. He had to be searching for Robert Wesley. "Oh, find him, my little friend," Millie whispered. "Please find him."

The front door slammed and Millie looked away from her mirror. She wanted to call out to Benjamin to come see. But for once, Millie exercised real patience. And just when she thought she couldn't wait another moment, Benjamin walked in.

"Benjamin, guess what? I saw Little Bitty Bird!" she declared.

"So, you saw Little Bitty Bird. What do you mean?" Benjamin asked.

"I saw him in my mirror!"

Benjamin picked up her gold-framed mirror and looked at it, not really understanding what Millie meant. His forehead puckered in a frown.

"Look carefully, Benjamin," Millie pleaded. "Don't you see the woods?"

"No, I don't see any woods. I just see my face!" He set the mirror down.

Millie let out an exasperated sigh. "Well, I saw a woods, and Little Bitty Bird was flying through it. And that means he's out there looking for Robert Wesley. I told you Little Bitty Bird would find Robert Wesley."

Benjamin sat down on the edge of Millie's bed and shook his head slowly. He looked at his little sister and spoke kindly. "Millie, you're really good at pretending, but maybe it isn't good to pretend so much."

Millie never had a chance to answer because Papa came in the room. And he had a "good idea" look on his face. Millie tried to appear interested in Papa's idea, but her thoughts were still with Little Bitty Bird and Robert Wesley.

"How would you two like to come with me on a pastoral visit?" Papa asked. "I must go visit the Powells, and I promised Mamma I'd pick up some fabric she ordered."

"Thanks, Papa," Benjamin replied, "but I really want to fly my kite some more."

"That's fine, Benjamin. But I'd enjoy your company, Miss Millicent. What do you say?" Millie knew that Dr. Neils wanted her to get out of the house. He said seeing new sights would lift her spirits and help her regain her strength. Ordinarily she would enjoy riding with Papa, but it was hard to take her mind off that scene in her mirror.

"Okay, Papa, I'll go," she reluctantly announced.

It was a treat to see the Powell farm. Millie stayed in the car while Papa went inside to visit Farmer Powell and his wife. Millie watched the dapple-gray mare frolic in a nearby pasture. But it seemed an eternity before Papa finally returned to the car. As they waved good-bye to the Powells, Millie noticed how old they looked. Was it because Robert Wesley was missing and all their sons were in the war?

As Papa drove toward town, Millie watched for familiar landmarks along the way. She used to walk along this same road on her way to school. That seemed so long ago now. And it didn't look like she'd be returning to school in the near future. How she wished that Little Bitty Bird would find Robert Wesley and come home. Then she could get to the Lemon Tree and the magical lemons would make her strong again!

Papa drove down Main Street, past the post office and the drugstore, and then parked in front of the fabric shop. He hoisted Millie onto his back and said, "It's about time you were out and about, Millie. You certainly don't want to be like a house plant, now do you?" Millie giggled. She could hardly picture herself a house plant!

Inside the shop, the clerk had Mamma's fabric all wrapped and waiting. While Papa exchanged a few pleasant words, Millie looked at the beautiful spring cottons that draped the walls behind the counter. Those heavy plaids and wools like Mamma had used to make Millie's school outfits were no longer displayed. Millie thought sadly about how those outfits had hung in the closet all winter. Then it was time to leave. Back in the car Millie thought of Little Bitty Bird and wondered if the picture in her mirror would show up again. She hoped so. "Be there again," she wished silently. "Please be there."

Back at home Millie was surprised to find Widow Long having tea with Mamma in the living room. Mamma insisted on having Papa and Millie join them. Normally Millie would have enjoyed having tea and cookies like an adult, but today it was agony to sit politely while she wondered what might be happening inside her mirror. Benjamin came inside with his kite tucked under his arm. He ignored Mamma's offer of a cookie and instead raced up the stairs to Millie's bedroom.

"That boy—he must have something on his mind!" Mamma frowned. Widow Long simply smiled as if she understood.

No sooner had Benjamin left than he returned to the living room. He looked at Millie with a strange expression on his face. "Millie," said Benjamin, "wouldn't you like to look in your Sunshine Box again? Maybe there's a gift to be opened today."

Millie didn't know what Benjamin meant, but she was certain that something was up, and she needed to get to her bedroom fast. If only she could race up those stairs in a hurry! Fortunately Papa seemed to understand, and he carried Millie up to her room. After Papa left, Millie asked, "What is it, Benjamin? Did you look in my mirror?"

Benjamin nodded. "I got to thinking maybe you really did see something in your mirror. So I came up here to look for myself. I didn't see anything, but look at this!" He handed the mirror to Millie. She peered inside, but the scene with the woods was gone. Then she noticed a small card with a picture of the Sunshine Box tied to its handle.

"Millie, I think this means you're supposed to look inside your Sunshine Box!" Benjamin exclaimed as he handed her the box. Millie pulled off lid and looked inside.

"Look—there's only one gift! There should be two. What's happened?" she asked.

"I don't know. Maybe you counted wrong," Benjamin said.

"No! I know there were two gifts." Millie felt confused.

"I think you should open the one gift just the same," urged Benjamin.

Millie lifted out what had been the largest gift of all. It was wrapped in yellow tissue paper and the card read "When the mirror tells you to open me, do so and make good use of what is inside." Millie hurried and opened the gift. It was a miniature Lemon Tree loaded down with tiny yellow lemons. She felt almost as surprised as when Little Bitty Bird had spoken for the first time.

She plucked off one of the lemons and popped it into her mouth. It tasted just like

the lemons from the Lemon Tree at the end of the magical tunnel! Did this mean she needed to work at getting strong again? Suddenly she remembered her brother. He had a curious look on his face. "Here, Benjamin, have one of my lemons!" she offered.

Suddenly her brow furrowed in thought. Only she and Little Bitty Bird knew about the other Lemon Tree. So just how did this miniature Lemon Tree get into her Sunshine Box? It really was a mystery.

Then a smile spread across her face. For some reason, seeing this little lemon tree reassured her that Little Bitty Bird must be on his way home. And surely he must be bringing them good news about Robert Wesley!

Chapter 14

A DAY OF MIRACLES

Tomorrow would be Easter Sunday. Three weeks had passed since Millie glimpsed Little Bitty Bird in the mirror, but there was still no sign of his return. She clung to a little piece of hope, not allowing herself to think that Robert Wesley was gone forever or that Little Bitty Bird would never return. She remembered the day when they'd received the awful news that Robert Wesley was missing. Papa had read part of Psalm 17 aloud. Millie still remembered the words "hide me under the shadow of Thy wings." Since that time Millie had prayed for Robert Wesley every day that God would keep him safe in the shadow of His wings. Remembering that Bible verse always kept a little ray of hope shining in Millie's heart.

With these thoughts rolling around in her head, Millie hopped out of bed, opened her bedroom window, and let the fragrant spring breeze caress her face. On the grassy hills beyond Widow Long's house, patches of pink and yellow wildflowers danced in the wind. The birds in the old maple tree beneath Millie's window chirped gaily as they swooped from branch to branch. Spring was finally here! What a wonderful time of year! God's world was waking up after the long winter's sleep.

Millie stretched and reached almost to the top of the window, enjoying the newly found strength in her arms and legs. She, too, was part of this grand awakening. Her ear was free of pain now, and it had been weeks since her head had throbbed. Several days ago Millie had surprised Mamma and Papa by walking down the stairs in time for breakfast. What fun it had been to surprise Dr. Neils! He was so pleased with her progress that he spoiled her with a huge cherry lollipop, and even Mamma didn't object.

One day when Anna Sue visited, she asked Millie about her miniature Lemon Tree that now stood bare of all of its fruit. Millie didn't think she could explain the secrets of her Sunshine Box to Anna Sue. Benjamin was the only person she'd ever tried to explain it to, and even he had difficulty accepting the mysterious events that were so real to Millie. Perhaps it was meant to be this way. Only Millie would know the wonders of the Sunshine Box—Millie and the mysterious person who had given her the box.

The early morning chill sent Millie skittering back into bed and under the warm covers. Lying there in the quiet house, Millie realized she was the only one awake. Her gaze traveled across the room to where the Sunshine Box sat upon her dresser. The Sunshine Box had surely been good medicine, cheering her on toward a complete recovery. Each gift had brought her happiness in different ways: Little Bitty Bird's friendship, the Fun Feather's mischievous tickling, beautiful scenes in the mirror, and delicious hot cocoa from the cup that mysteriously refilled itself when she wished for more. And, of course, the miniature Lemon Tree had provided the energy-giving fruit that helped her grow well and strong. One gift had not been opened. It was the one that had disappeared. Though Benjamin and Millie searched and searched, it was nowhere to be found. Even Mamma and Papa expressed concern over this strange loss. Millie remembered the gift well. It had been the smallest gift, wrapped in white tissue paper. Its tag said, "Last and best." Millie still believed that she would somehow find that gift.

But a bigger mystery than the disappearance of the last gift continued to nag her. Who had given her the marvelous, mysterious Sunshine Box? Would she ever know?

Clunking and banging in the next room told her that Benjamin was up. In the next minute he was somehow dressed and flying down the stairs toward the back door.

Millie jumped out of her own bed and followed. "Where are you going?"

"Over to Farmer Powell's barn," he called back. "I want to see if Robert Wesley's mare had her foal last night. Yesterday Farmer Powell told Papa he was sure she was getting ready to deliver. Get your clothes on if you want to come along."

"No, I don't think so, Benjamin. It would make me too sad to be there with Robert Wesley gone. I'll go see it when he comes home."

"You mean if he comes home, Millie."

"Don't you think he's coming home, Benjamin? You're not giving up, are you?"

"No, I wouldn't do that…it's just that this war scares me. Three soldiers from our church have already been killed. But I haven't given up on Robert Wesley. Like Papa says, we need to pray for him. Right now I want to see his new foal. He'd want me to see it if he were home. Tell Mamma I'll be back in time for breakfast."

Millie stood on the back stoop and watched as Benjamin ran across the backyard and through the field behind Widow Long's house to the meadow at the edge of the Powell farm. As Benjamin disappeared, she prayed again for Robert Wesley. "Little Bitty Bird must find him—he must!" she said out loud. She looked up above the hills and willed Little Bitty Bird to return with good news of Robert Wesley, but there was nothing but blue sky and white fluffy clouds as far as she could see.

Suddenly Millie realized that she wasn't the only one peering over the morning landscape. Right next door, Widow Long was leaning out her dining-room window looking up at the sky, squinting against the glare of the morning sun. Then, as if she'd failed to find what she was looking for, the old widow shook her head. Noticing Millie on the back stoop, the widow waved, then ducked back inside.

"I wonder," Millie said to herself, "what Widow Long was looking for? Could she have been looking for Little Bitty Bird too?"

Papa's voice interrupted her thoughts. "Millie, what are you doing out here with no wraps? You don't want to catch cold and miss the Easter service tomorrow. Come now, back inside with you!"

Shortly before breakfast Benjamin returned from Farmer Powell's. "The little filly is so cute," he told Millie. "She has three white stockings and a white star on her forehead. Farmer Powell said I might help train her when she's a little older. Normally that would be Robert Wesley's job, but..." his voice trailed off.

"I'm not giving up hope, Benjamin, and neither should you," Millie replied. "After all, Easter is a season of miracles!"

Benjamin grinned. "I bet there will be so many flowers this year that it'll be a miracle if we can see Papa behind the pulpit!"

Millie giggled. It would be funny to see poor Papa hidden by the many lavish flower arrangements! She and Benjamin walked to the church to see if they could help. This was Millie's first long walk, and oh, how good it felt! When they arrived at the church, several women were arranging flowers in vases. Millie gasped in surprise at the number of flowers that people had already brought to the church.

Millie loved Easter lilies best of all. They were so white—like drops of snow. And the trumpet-shaped flowers fairly shouted, "Jesus is risen!" as their fragrance filled the church with all the sweetness of spring. The organist added to the festive atmosphere as he practiced all the familiar Easter hymns. Just then, the old oak door of the church opened and in came Farmer Powell carrying the most beautiful Easter lily. Millie was worried that Easter might be sad for the Powells with all their sons gone to war and Robert Wesley missing. But the farmer's face broke into a radiant smile as he walked directly to the front of the church and placed his gorgeous lily right in front of the pulpit, smack in the middle of the other lilies. Then he simply nodded and quietly departed.

Millie puzzled over that for a moment. She knew that Easter meant victory over death. So if Robert Wesley had been killed (which she stubbornly refused to believe) he would still be alive in heaven. But Millie wanted him to be alive here on earth and to come back to all who loved him. So, while she wasn't completely sad, she wasn't perfectly happy either.

That evening Mamma helped Millie lay out her best clothes for Easter morning. "This is the happiest time of year," Mamma said as she kissed Millie good-night.

"I know, Mamma, but I want Robert Wesley to come home." Millie fought back tears. She prayed once more for her friend's safe return, then fell asleep.

Easter morning dawned with a clear, cloudless sky of brilliant blue. Millie stretched and marveled again at how good it felt to be well. Easter joy washed over her. Something good was going to happen today—something special, something wonderful!

Millie was the first one out of bed. She was filled with such a sense of anticipation that she quietly crept down the stairs and stepped out onto the stoop. It was then that she first heard the music. Very faint and far away. Her whole body tingled with the sound. She stood perfectly still, as if any movement would stop that wonderful music. She listened intently, certain that it was coming from—a dulcimer! It seemed so strange, so impossible, and yet it sounded so wonderfully real. The lilting melody seemed to beckon, and she had no choice but to follow. She hurried across the stone path, through the rose arbor, over the fence, and into the cherry orchard.

The music drew her on until it seemed as if she could almost touch it. Then she saw him. He sat upon the fence at the edge of the meadow. Millie shook her head in amazement. Were her eyes playing tricks on her? No! He was really there. Robert Wesley had come home! She ran as hard as she could. He was alive! It was an Easter miracle! After all this time God had answered their prayers.

"Robert Wesley, Robert Wesley, you've come home! You've come home!" Millie cried as she ran toward him.

"Millie!" he shouted. He set his dulcimer into the soft meadow grass. "Just look at you. Now, aren't you a sight!" He scooped her up in an enormous hug, then laughed his big contagious laugh. Tears of joy streamed down Millie's cheeks as she stared at him.

"You're home, you're home!" she repeated. "I sent Little Bitty Bird to find you. He was looking for you in a forest."

Robert Wesley gave her a look of surprise. "I was in a forest for a long time," he explained. "There was a terrible battle and I was hit in my leg."

Millie gasped and looked at his leg.

He smiled. "I have a pretty good limp, but I'm just fine, Millie. After I was injured, I got separated from the others and had to hide in the forest for three long days. Finally a farmer found me. He and his wife hid me and took care of me. It was a terrible risk, but they saved my life. When I was strong enough to travel, they took me to the Red Cross. I just got home yesterday, but Mom and Dad thought we should save the big surprise for the Easter Sunday service."

"Now I know why your father looked so happy when he brought his lily to the church yesterday. Oh, I'm just so glad you're home!"

Robert Wesley smiled a mischievous grin. "Well, you know, Millie, I had to come back so I could give you the last gift from your Sunshine Box."

Millie's mouth dropped open. He reached into his jacket pocket and pulled out a small box

wrapped in white tissue paper. She speechlessly read the tag: "Last and best." Still grinning, Robert Wesley added, "I'm sorry you had to wait so long for this one."

"Oh, my!" Millie whispered, too overwhelmed to even say thank you. Trembling with excitement, she quickly unwrapped the small gift. But when she opened it there was nothing, absolutely nothing inside. She blinked and looked up at her friend.

"Hmm," said Robert Wesley thoughtfully. "You see, this last gift is too special to fit into a box. Close your eyes for a moment."

Millie obeyed. Then Robert Wesley gently kissed her on the forehead. "You see, Millie, the best gift is love."

Millie beamed up at him. "So you're the one who gave me my Sunshine Box, Robert Wesley!"

"Well, I helped, but it was really Widow Long's idea. After hearing one of her stories from long ago, I decided that a Sunshine Box might be just the thing to help you get well. So the widow and I teamed up. Remember the note on your mirror? Widow Long put it there so you would find the Lemon Tree. And it was Widow Long who took this last little gift out of the Sunshine Box so I could give it to you myself."

"But Robert Wesley, what about the magic in the gifts?" Millie asked.

"The magic? What magic?" Robert Wesley asked with a puzzled look.

"You know—the Fun Feather that tickled me and the mirror that showed me beautiful scenes. And what about the cocoa that was always in the cup? And where did you get the Lemon Tree that helped me get strong again?"

Then suddenly Millie remembered Little Bitty Bird and she cried out, "Oh, and Robert Wesley, what about Little Bitty Bird? Where is he? I've been so worried. Little Bitty Bird is alive, isn't he?"

"Alive? You mean the toy bird that was your first gift?" Robert Wesley asked.

Suddenly Millie thought she heard a peep, and it seemed to come from inside Robert Wesley's pocket. Millie laughed and jumped with excitement. Then Robert Wesley put his hand in his pocket and pulled out Little Bitty Bird.

"Oh, Little Bitty Bird!" cried Millie with joy.

"Hmm," Robert Wesley said with a wink. "How did this bird get into my pocket?"

"See, the gifts must be magic," said Millie hopefully. "Oh, how did you do it, Robert Wesley? Please tell me."

Robert Wesley smiled. "Millie, the only magic that Widow Long and I put in the Sunshine Box was love—God's love. Love is the strongest power in the world, and it helped to make you well again. Even if we don't understand everything, we can all be very thankful. And I'm sure thankful to be home from the war and to find my Millie girl all well and strong. God's love did all that!"

Millie nodded. She was thankful. She still didn't understand everything about the Sunshine Box. Was the magic real or had she just dreamed of it? Or, as Benjamin had suggested, had she been pretending? Perhaps she would never know. At least she knew that the Sunshine Box was a gift of love.

"And now I'd better get back home if I'm to make it to the Easter service on time," announced Robert Wesley with a bright sunny smile.

The warm spring wind ruffled her hair as she watched Robert Wesley pick up his dulcimer and walk toward the Powell farm. Millie studied Little Bitty Bird, now perched on her finger. Suddenly she thought she knew just what he was thinking. And although he didn't speak out loud, she could imagine him saying the words. "Millie girl, there's more to the Sunshine Box than anyone knows." She smiled and stroked his tawny brown feathers with her fingertip.

Then Little Bitty Bird winked one round eye, and Millie was certain she heard him say, "But I'll never tell, Millie. I'll never tell!"